Improvisation Rites: from John Cage's 'Song Books' to the Scratch Orchestra's 'Nature Study Notes'. Collective practices 2011 – 2017

An exploration by Stefan Szczelkun

Nature Study Notes - Improvisation Rites 1969 - 2017

ISBN 978-1-870736-96-1

Published in London 2018 by Routine Art Co.

Printed and Distributed by IngramSpark UK

Routine Art Co is a umbrella name I use for collaborative projects

CONTENTS

Introduction

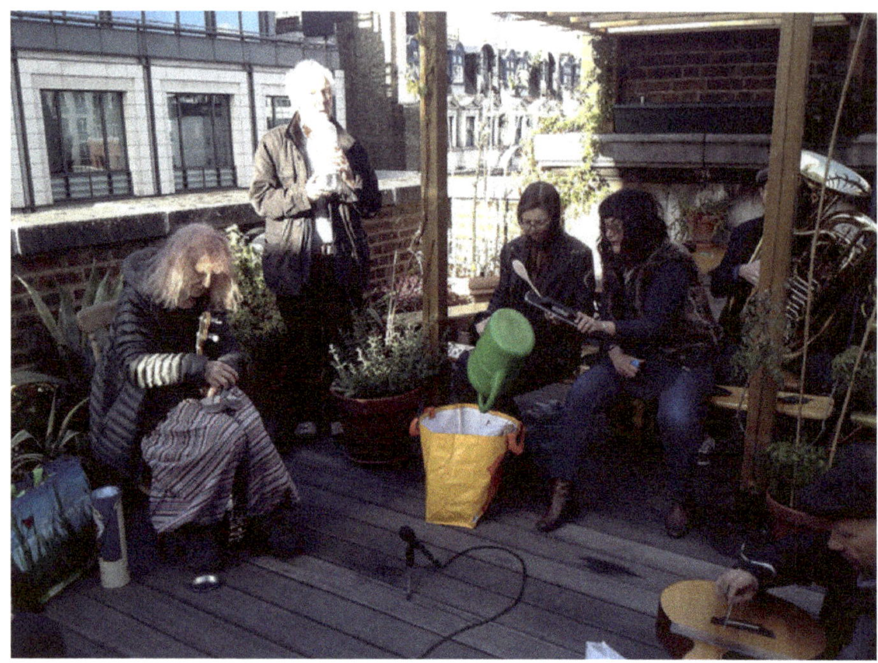

The importance of Collective 'Free' Improvisation

1. I had been much inspired by being part of the original Scratch Orchestra and in 2012 decided to revisit its foundational document, The *Nature Study Notes* collection of improvisation rites, with a new generation of performers, alongside some older members of the original collective. This was conceived as a hands-on way of learning about a key part of British music history. By 2017 it had become something even more exciting.

2. I wanted to start by exploring an aspect of cultural history that this project arose from - in particular the influence of John Cage, using his magnum opus 'Song Books'.

3. I hope to elucidate why I think that these experiments with collective improvisation are significant.

4. This book is an account of this process using archival materials.

High Art music became the bourgeois self-image. In its orchestral forms, it represented the power of the captains of industry as they conducted their workers to ever grander achievements. But at core, bourgeois culture is literary and written, and published forms of language control or mediate other high art forms. The 'written' score by a genius composer was used to discipline and make a controlled aesthetic form from the skills of the ensemble of workers.

This form ossified into a rigid canon of 'the classics' by the early 20th century, but also became globalised with the worldwide spread of Western models of capitalism. Every city That want to be a player on the world stage has to have its concert hall and orchestra to make itself acceptable to the jet-setting capitalist class. In the early twentieth-century orchestral music's development fractured as the limits of tonality were reached and popular music became an electrified commodity. The gradual global spread of demands for democracy also challenged the relevance of the hierarchical authoritarian forms of 'classical' music.

John Cage suggested we 'start from scratch', listening to the sounds that emanate from the world. With others, he reinvented the score using a wide range of graphic marks. But it was Cornelius Cardew who decisively challenged the hierarchical form of the orchestra and concert with the Scratch Orchestra, that he started in 1969. Although there was a core of dedicated classically-trained musicians, anybody could join and 'play'. The scores were made to be accessible to anyone, and the concerts were organised by the youngest members first. I will say more in Chapter 3.

In the Scratch Orchestra of 1969 we were able to collectively express our inner world with a startling degree of freedom. It was a fantastically liberating feeling at the time. But amazingly, using similar approaches nearly 50 years later, in Athens Greece, the liberating effect was palpably similar.

The initial idea for the recent project was to work with a younger generation of improvising performers to transmit the Scratch Orchestra praxis by doing it rather than by reading about it. A group of original Scratch members worked alongside me with a larger group of invited younger artists. We met and discussed things over a long period to create something of the feel of the 'original' Scratch Orchestra.

I see the significance of improvisation in large groups as important because it parallels a larger process of cultural formation. It is a microcosm of the symbolic exchanges that we make whenever we are 'playing' together. Improvisation tries to find ideal conditions of creativity, interactivity, empathy and listening that might make for a more dynamic, and less authoritarian kind of society. It allows people to experience the power of joining their inner desires in a process from which a collective form comes into being.

The aim of this book

This book attempts to reproduce material that was close to the process that we went through together, by using the emails and other ephemeral writings by me and other members of the group. It is meant to give an insight into processes rather than providing a gloss on final appearances. The feel is partly of an archival narrative collage.

I hope the book is accessible to people who don't know the Scratch Orchestra, as well as those who were involved in some part of the process described. We started our exploration with a composer who, came before Cardew and broke the mould of orchestral music making - John Cage. There is a description of both the scores that were used. 'Song Books' is one of John Cage's main scores, and 'Nature Study Notes' is the set of verbal scores that was at the heart of the Scratch Orchestra from its inception in 1969.

Acknowledgements

Thanks to Howard Slater for early editorial work on organising material and giving it a rough shape. Thank you, Ali Warner for giving the whole a consistent formatting design and for copy-editing the first half with unearthly precision. Thank you, Carole Finer for all the supportive radio shows she made in this period. Then, there is the marvellous performance photography by Martin Dixon, Deidre McGale, Emmanuelle Waeckerle and Stathis Mamalakis. Thanks to Bryn Harris for audio recording most of the performances. Recordings which cannot of course be included in this paper book.

Photographs without credits were taken by the author.

Chapter 1

John Cage's 'Song Books'

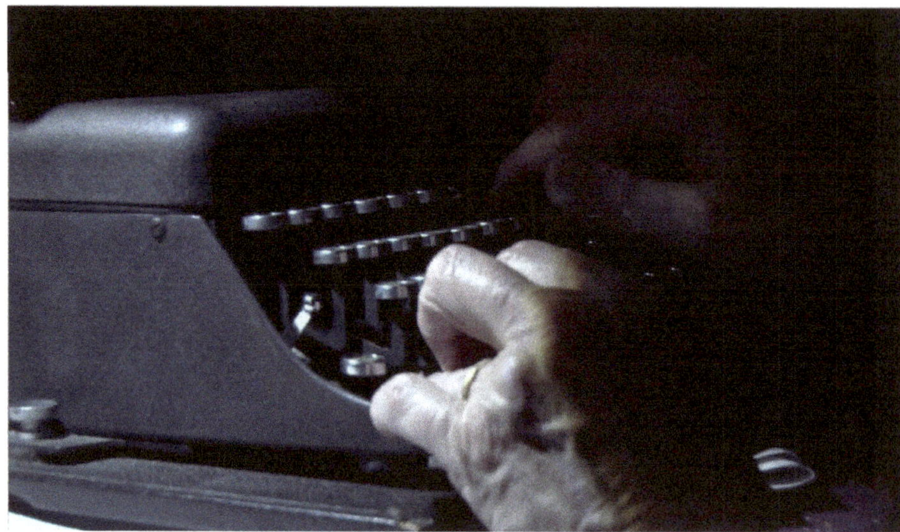

Carol Finer performing Song Books at Cafe Oto

John Cage's 'Song Books' 1970

My aim, with the project documented here, was to find a way to explore the Scratch Orchestra's improvisation rites from the late Sixties with a new generation of performers. So why start with John Cage (1912-1992)? One reason was that Cage was better known than Cornelius Cardew (1936-1981), founder of the Scratch Orchestra, and the year of our proposed performance was the centenary of Cage's birth so there was widespread public awareness. Cage was prior to Cardew in establishing certain performative modes that the Scratch Orchestra then developed in a radical and more political direction. The deeper reason for doing this double-barrelled project was that I'd observed that, as the modernist music of this period was reprised, it was being drained of its original unpredictability and performance art edge. It was a trend that was happening across the board. I include a review of one highly-disciplined and precise performance of 'Song Books' to illustrate my point, for those interested.

Description of Cage's magnum opus

'Song Books' is a collection of 90 separate solos for voice arranged in two volumes. It was published by Editions Peters in 1970, with another slim volume of instructions and additional material. Each volume was bound along the short edge with a plastic comb-binding. The set cost over £100 which thankfully my workplace, the University of Westminster, paid for.

Cage's directions stipulate that the solos can be performed with or without other indeterminate music, and that they can be used by one or more singers in any order and be superimposed or repeated. To complicate the idea of *a song,* some of the solos are directives for theatrical activity. In fact, there are four categories of solo: straightforward vocal song, song using electronics, song as a instruction for theatrical action, and theatre with electronics. Each of the solos is marked as relevant or irrelevant to the subject: "We connect Satie with Thoreau."

Singers are directed *not* to co-ordinate the programmes that they make with other performers e.g. "Any resultant silence is not to be feared." Performers are told not to respond spontaneously to juxtapositions that occur by chance i.e. "They should continue to perform their programme, come what may".

I was intrigued by the instruction to 'connect Satie with Thoreau'. Each song is marked a REVELANT or IRRELEVANT to this notion. It implies a cognisance of the rich transatlantic background of both John Cage and modernist experimental culture and its connection to utopian thought.

Henry Thoreau (1817-1862) was born and lived in Concord, Massachusetts, USA. Erik Satie (1866-1925) was born in Honfleur in Northern France, and lived in Monmartre, Paris.

This is sometimes directly referenced in the individual songs, e.g. In Solo 30 a text collaged from Thoreau's Journal is given conventional musical notation. The first two lines from Solo 42 are also quoted from Thoreau:

> "Wasps are building; Summer squashes; Saw a fish hawk, when I hear this; both bush-es and trees are thin-ly leaved; Few ripe ones on sand-y banks; Rose right up high in to the air."

Another long, conventionally notated piece quotes from the first paragraph of Thoreau's 'Essay on Civil Disobedience' (Solo 34 and 35). The score of Solo 5 is an simply an engraving of Thoreau's face. We are instructed to "Wander over the portrait of Thoreau so that the path taken suggests a melodic line." Bron Jones is here, shown performing the face of Thoreau.

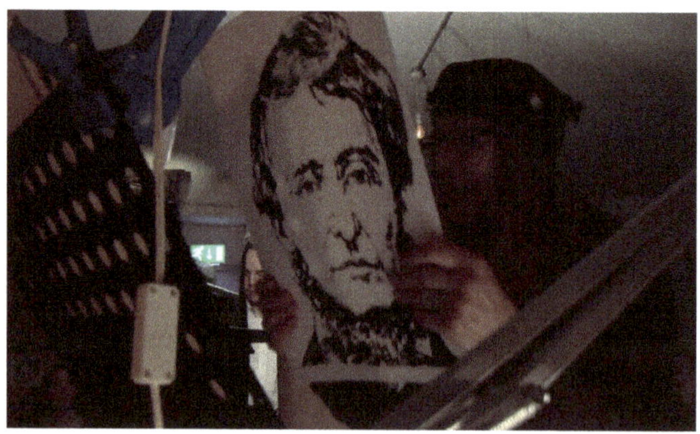

A text by Erik Satie, used in Solo for Voice 43, is presented with a varied typography reminiscent of the Concrete Poetry of the time i.e. "**et tOUT CELA M'Est advenu PAR LA FAUTE DE la musique.**" (And all this happened to me through the fault of Music.) Four different versions of the same text are presented, and we can imagine Cage hard at work with his Letraset.

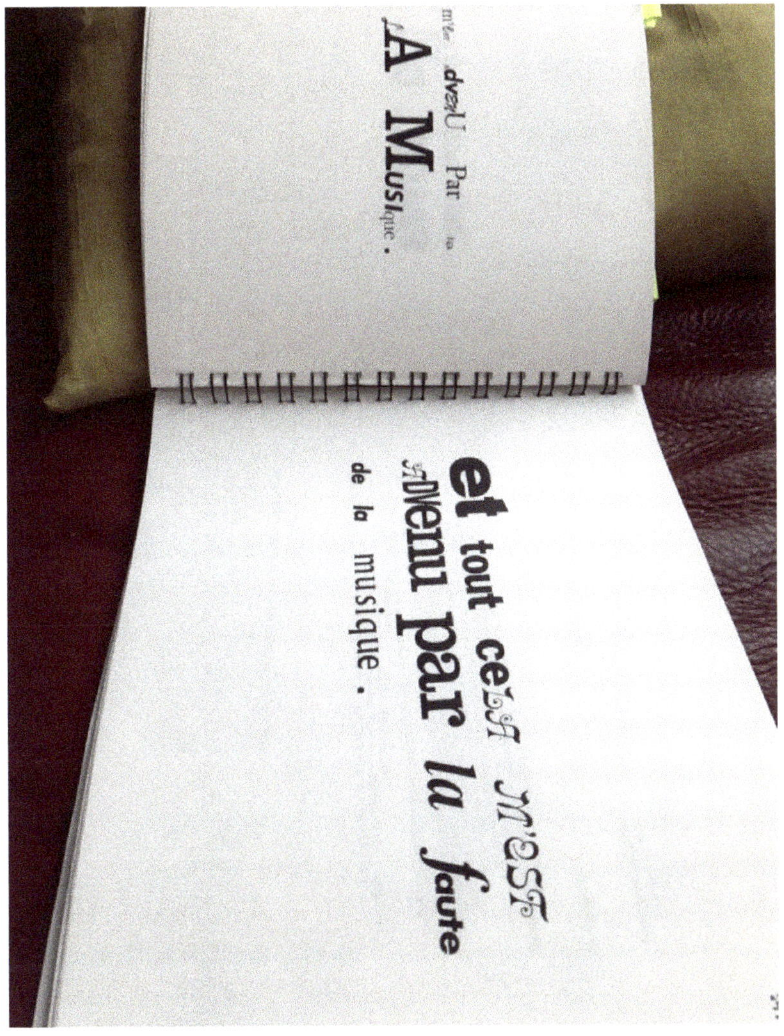

The solos vary from very simple instructions to a whole range of graphic scores that were cutting edge at the time. Examples of verbal instructions are:

SOLO FOR VOICE 78, THEATRE (IRRELEVANT)

DIRECTIONS

What can you do?
"I can take off my shoes and put them on."

SOLO FOR VOICE 51, THEATRE WITH ELECTRONICS (RELEVANT)

DIRECTIONS

Play a recording of a forest fire.

Beginning to organise a group

During the preparations for getting a large ensemble together to perform John Cage's 'Song Books' – in itself a warm-up before performing The Scratch Orchestra's 'Nature Study Notes' – Peter Ellison alerted me to a recently announced rendition of the 'Song Books' by the Exaudi Group at King's Place.

Stefan's email to Peter Ellison (early in 2011)

Thanks for alerting me to this Peter ... Yes, we must try to go!! Never heard of King's Place before! Eeek! the establishment have got to 'Song Books' first!! Interesting that a previewer, Christopher Fox, referenced Trevor Wishart's work with voice. (Wishart had been an occasional 'Slippery Merchant', our anarchic sub-group within the Scratch Orchestra.) Fox basically goes on to argue: "The Song Books work best when the balance is firmly tipped in favour of virtuosity, so that the more theatrical actions become incidental to the overall vocal spectacle." He goes on to talk about Cage's theatre instructions that he thinks are overly easy to perform.

This seems a mild statement, but in here hides the whole of the establishment ideology of exclusion; of drawing hard edges to valid aesthetic creation within an area of excellence, discipline and virtuosity. We would have to discuss the form of discipline implied to make full sense of this. He marks the virtuosity of the trained singers above the aesthetic and joy of ordinary actions – I can't think that Cage would have approved of this.

I invited the first younger generation improviser to show interest, Ali Warner, to come along.

Ali Warner's email to Stefan

An unexpected next step in our project! I went to King's Place for the first time recently (for an acapella voice festival) and I actually didn't enjoy it as a venue, as it is vast, cavernous and modern, so doesn't feel very hospitable inside.

They tried to put a trio of female voices on in the foyer (mezzanine balcony) – one singer couldn't see above the barrier rail – and they were drowned out by all the noise that a large hard-surface space with high ceilings and lots of people creates.

The concert halls themselves seemed good - lots of wood and quite an intimate feeling. I noticed on the website that 'Kings Place won Business Venue of the Year at the 2010 Visit London Awards' which might say something about the tenor of the place. But they seem to have interesting programming, I just didn't find it very welcoming.

In terms of the Guardian article, I found that Cage's original quoted remark (freedom versus 'foolishness') spoke to me in terms of what I have been experiencing myself in explorations with form & formlessness, and I thought it was a good one to raise – however I don't think the writer's conclusion that 'therefore we need virtuosity' is the only or correct one. What is would be worthy of more discussion!

Stefan, could you bring the Songbooks score or copies with you? (or do you think it would be inappropriate to refer to them during the performance!) I will also tell any singers I am in touch with, and it would be good to be able to make contact with the singers you have mentioned if they are able to come."

Chapter 1 Section 1

A review of John Cage's 'Song Books' (1970) by Exaudi, King's Place, London, 28 March 2011

The performance space was a flat studio about 20 metres square, with a black curtain and a stage on one side. The seating was in rows of moveable chairs and the singers were arranged on the stage, to the side of the stage, and to the rear of the stage. The evening was sold out for this rare performance.

The performers were dressed as we might expect with 'serious' music, they looked like bank clerks without their jackets and ties on. The electronics man, Bill Thompson, had his shirt hanging out. One man in black had dreadlocks. But who was the character with the big furry hat on stage looking at his MacBook? About half-way through the hour-long performance a technician joined him on stage as if something had gone wrong with whatever the laptop was in charge of. Later he walked off as if in a huff. Had something gone wrong? The Cage masterwork was rather crammed into the hour, and I wondered if this was because they were aiming to make a CD. There was a gap in the market for a recording of 'Song Books'. Also, the performance, which was polished, seemed to have a rehearsed feel to it. The random juxtaposition of pieces seemed to go all too smoothly with few lulls or cacophonic pile-ups that we might have expected. The score isn't smooth, its all bitty with variegations of textures. In the catalogue, James Weeks, Exaudi's director, describes the scored songs as beautiful, which is strange because they often seem quite ugly compared to, say, the graphics of Cardew's 'Treatise'. Certainly, Cage is no great graphic artist, but that's not the point anyway.

Why was it so smooth? Why shouldn't it be smooth? The professionalism of the troupe is not in question. What is in question is whether a professional sort of discipline can give us a satisfactory rendition of 'Song Books' which is comprised of 48 scores needing various levels of musical ability, and 42 instructions for 'theatre'. The need for perfect timing and pitch dominated the visuality, with stopwatches hanging like medallions and tuning forks struck on knees to intone a song. The actual theatre-half of the concert was tastefully kept on table tops that were hardly visible to most of the audience. The visual impact of the concert was perhaps just 5%. Of course, if your aim is to make a CD that's understandable, but might more overt theatre performances have dislodged the cosy safety of the delicate virtuoso singing? But couldn't this also have meant that the CD would have had a bit more edge, danger, excitement? A bit more feeling for the era of its creation in 1970 and 'the space between Satie and Thoreau', that half of the pieces are meant to be enacted within, was needed. Seventies radicalism was a distant prospect here, despite the anarchist song being repeated at least 3 times in some nice, if subdued, variations: expressing that 'The best form of government is no government at all'.

The troupe's dress-code reminded me of an administrative centre. It felt like 'Song Books' had been administrated for the new millennium, and in time to be on sale in the shops by Cage anniversary in 2012. Certainly, commodification and comfort were words that came to mind.

The other thing that spoilt it for me was the use of

microphones on stands to render vocals for electronic modulation. The scores just say 'with electronics' or not. This doesn't mean that the voice has to be wholly modulated. The microphone stands emphasised the fixity and anal rigidity of it all (and anyway, I hate unnecessary amplification of the human voice as it is so reductive).

To be fair, there were moments of loveliness which you might not guess from my diatribe! The babel of voices near to the end, that came out from an earlier linguistically impenetrable libretto, seemed to be very relevant to the London of today, with its many spoken languages. But even such moments didn't save it from trampling on the memory of John Cage, rather than investigating what he meant when he said that he wanted to 'start from scratch'.

Kings Place itself intones an atmosphere of professionalism and mental hygiene. It is a corporate environment, in which art is gathered to provide a throne for The Guardian Newspaper which seems to inhabit the upper reaches of the building. The space inveigles against the cultural freedom that I always imagined that Cage was reaching out for. With ultra-professionalism comes a pretentiousness and discipline that curtails the human spirit. It is perhaps a danger inherent in such scores. But anyway, it's not a home for the live and living avant-garde. When Ali sung a workers' folk song on the way out it was like a breath of fresh air, making us realise what a conditioned environment we had been in.

A central problem of realising 'Song Books' is whether you do a retro version, or try to realise it with contemporary idioms. Do you actually use an old typewriter for its clickety-clackety sounds? Do you evoke 'the space between Thoreau and Satie' as Cage asks of his performers in his introduction. In other words, to consider the 'space' between the European and the North American avant-gardes, or do you think of what is today's equivalent?

Ali Warner to Stefan and Peter

I think this is a perceptive review – at first, I was surprised when you dived straight into the practicalities (although perhaps this is the theatre/staging perspective that we reflected was not so in evidence in that production), and at the same time I liked the way you brought out the furry hat affair so early on – this was figural for me! By the end of the review, you really have touched on all the key points of the experience for me, plus shed some new light – referencing the all-important stopwatches (and the singer that we thought looked like Samantha Cameron who had a habit of checking the watch on her inside wrist too), the high-point of vocal layering near the end, the description of the building 'intoning… mental hygiene' - brilliant! Plus, The Guardian in the upper-reaches/ fresh air vs. air-conditioning - this applies to the sound quality as well as the air, I think.

I noticed that about the typewriter too – it almost seemed out of place, i.e. something else would have met Cage's instruction better – particularly given how many powerbooks were in evidence!

Lovely to meet you, Peter, and hope to get more chance to talk to you at our next meeting. Stefan - I have the article for you that I mentioned, and will try to get it copied to send. I really enjoyed our conversation (by the way, do you have any interest in going to see the Laurie Anderson exhibition at the Barbican?). Look forward to continuing to be in touch with you both.

Chapter 1 Section 2

Song Books: Organisation and Process

A group of performers wanting to take part in the project gradually built up, almost entirely through word of mouth and recommendation from original Scratch members. The original Scratch people at that time in 2011 were myself, Peter Ellison, Carole Finer, Carolyn Rogers and John Tilbury. The younger new people that had confirmed an interest were: Bron Jones (former singer in Crass performing as Eve Libertine), Ali Warner, Renate Biruls, Sharon Gal, Portia Winters, Robbie Lockwood and Lucy Galland.

Around the same time, I met Hamish from Cafe Oto in North London and sensed he was interested in the project, I had been writing to him but hadn't heard back. After months, I finally got a positive offer and we decided to take a date on Sunday 11 March in the following year. Not the most popular evening slot, but it was a 'no money up front for a share of the door money' deal and we had no funding. Now we had something real to aim for.

Stefan Szczelkun's email to the group

Dear Song Books peoples! In an hour, I am going to send an email to Hamish at Cafe Oto to confirm Sunday 11 March 2012 as the date for our first performance of 'Song Books'. I'm really pleased to be able to finally confirm a date! I feel we have a powerful core group now, and we can expand it if we wish. For the next few months, I think it best if we concentrate on forming our own ensemble approaches and, if possible, meeting each other - even if only incrementally. Feel free to take initiatives to create meetings or communicate with each other.

I'm going to Oto on the evening of Tuesday 21 June for the launch of the Paul Burwell memorial book – if anyone is interested, please do join me. Then Ali, Bron, Carol and I are going to meet at Oto for a lunchtime discussion on Sunday 17 July – let's say 1–3pm. Unfortunately, Robbie and Peter may not be able to make that, but it's the best we can do. This meeting should, I think, concentrate on thinking about the singing.

We will need to find one or more electronics performers. There are several possibilities - no rush. There is also the question of recording a radio broadcast on Resonance FM (Carol Finer has a regular programme).

Stefan to Ali and the group

Hi Ali, yes, maybe it's good if the main people with singing skills can all meet on the 17th - that's only four in all. I think it's good if they can meet me - and Carole Finer - at this early stage as well. You core singers need to be in charge of how you approach the score; the distribution of songs; how long the performance should be; whether to use your idea of wearing numbers relating to the song you are doing; how you appear in publicity; how the songs chosen appear in publicity or not; how you want to use the space in Cafe Oto; what the meaning of the space between Satie and Thoreau is; how the electronics should be conducted, etc. etc. And you can all look through the whole score, which I will bring along. We probably need to end up with twice as many singers by February, but if the core has decided some basic strategies then the others can probably fall in with this.

Stefan to the group

The next 'Song Books' meet-up is on Tuesday 20 September, 6.30pm-9pm, at Madame Lillie's in Stoke Newington, N16 6BD (I have no surviving record of our improvisation session).

I've realised that the photo-portraits I took with a GoPro camera are a complete distraction from what we're doing. So I won't use them or put them online. Thanks for the feedback (people hated them!).

I will be available in my office at 32 Wells Street, W1T 3UW for score study sessions on Thursday 21st 10.30am-4pm, Tuesday 26th 2-4.30pm, Thursday 28th 10.30am-4pm and Wednesday 3rd August in the morning. It is better if two or more people can come together. Maybe Ali can co-ordinate?

Minutes of the meeting starting in Cafe Oto (30 October 2011)

Present: Bron, Carole, Stefan, Portia, Renate & Geri (Robbie and Lucy visited briefly for the start of the meeting in Cafe Oto). Apologies were received from Ali, Carolyn and Peter.

The main ingredients were:

1. Robbie and Lucy introducing themselves and the idea of them making video documentations that might take some part in the performance. I think they will contact Bron and Portia to shoot some process footage, as they live in the area. They then left Cafe Oto to do a job.

2. Next, we had a lovely autumnal walk from Cafe Oto through the backstreets of Dalston and Butterfield Green to Bron's beautiful studio space. When we arrived there, we tried out Portia's home-made contact mikes and had tea. Then Bron gave a talk on Thoreau, which gave us more insight into Cage than some of us had

expected. Hopefully she will write up her notes so others can share this. Portia will do her talk on Satie next time.

3. Geri then arrived, and we discussed her proposal that the performance should be 'durational' rather than an intense 60 -100 minutes. A good discussion without a very definite conclusion. Probably we will do a conventional performance length, without interval, at Oto. Time to be determined when we have all got further in deciding which of the songs we want to perform. Perhaps we could follow up with a durational performance at Goldsmiths College in Spring 2012? It was suggested we each draw up a poster of the scores we are doing - only to be unveiled at the actual performance (as we are not meant to co-ordinate our individual programmes).

4. I have been wrong in promoting the idea of a chance arrangement of each of our pieces. What the general instructions actually say is: "Given two or more singers, each should make an independent program, not fitted or related in a predetermined way to anyone else's program. Any resultant silence in a program is not to be feared. Simply perform as you had decided to, before you knew what would happen." (John Cage, from the 'General Directions' in 'Song Books', Oct 1970)

Later Note: Is this a key difference between Cage and Cardew? Cage preferred chance operations whereas Cardew was for rational choice.

5. I made a suggestion, with which people generally concurred, that we should not try to meet again this year as an ensemble. This does not mean people should not meet individually to try out stuff e.g. Geri and Ali to meet up with Grundik? Portia and Renate to meet up with Ali? Robbie and Lucy to meet Bron etc. Then we should have two quite long meetings in the run-up to the Oto

performance in March next year. The best dates seem to be the Sunday January 29th, and February 26th. But if you can't do either of these, please indicate other Sundays in between that you could do.

Basic arrangement: to meet at Oto at 1pm and work until at least 5pm, possibly eating together in the early evening.

Civil disobedience at every opportunity, please.

P.S. We need a publicity image or photo. Anyone got any ideas?

Stefan to the group

How about this photo as a holding publicity shot for the Cafe Oto website?

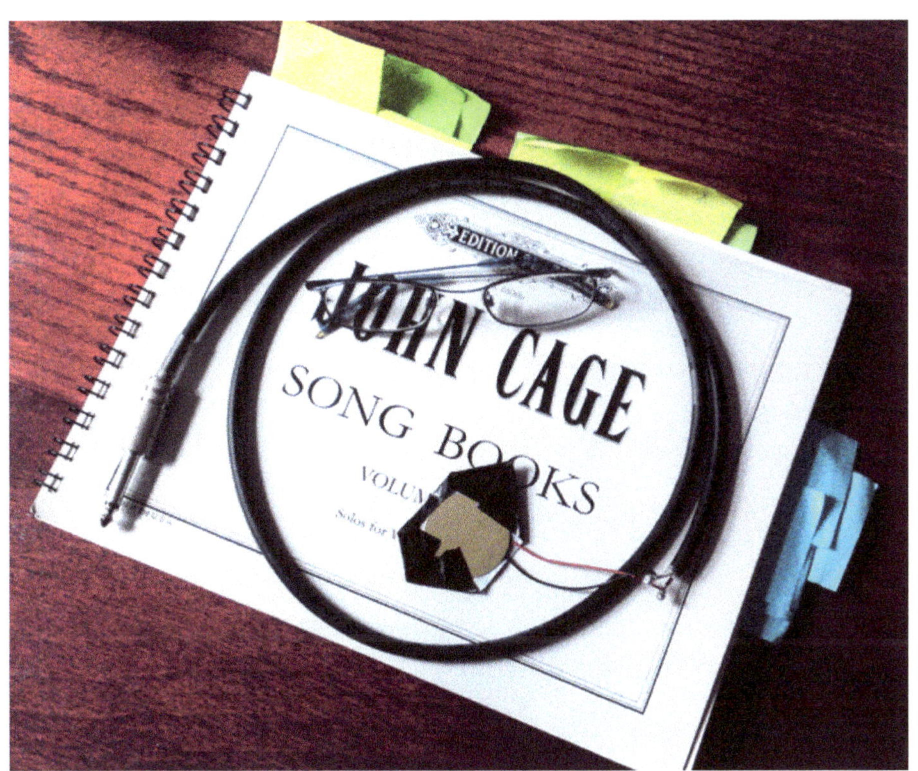

Portia Winters to the group

How's the civil disobedience going? It was a beautiful meeting. I'm looking forward to the concert in March. Also looking forward to hooking up elsewhere with anyone who fancies it.

I'm reading Walden at the moment, and very much enjoying it. It's also tying into a project I'm working on with recordings from my garden; of the environmental drones and hums, the trees/leaves/fridges/aeroplanes etc., and the singing of resonant frequencies found within these recordings.

The re-reflections of Thoreau's interests through this other project are linking together in the head for me with the sensibilities of the performance structure of Cage's voiceworks, and I'm finding in my thoughts an interesting leap between the centuries.

"If a man does not keep pace with his companions, perhaps it is because he hears a different drummer. Let him step to the music which he hears, however measured or far away." (Thoreau) And [play] as a response to environmental and media-voice saturations of daily experiences here and now.

Autumn leaves! They're EVERYWHERE at the moment.

John Tilbury to Stefan

Dear Stefan, an apology. I'm so sorry. You are on my list of invitees to a soiree in Finsbury Park, but somehow, I omitted to contact you. It's a performance of a late Beckett novella, 'Worstward Ho'. I have pre-recorded the text and accompany myself live at the piano. It's something I have been working on for a few years now, finally come to fruition. It's tomorrow, Saturday, 6.30pm for 7. Lasts 80 minutes so will be finished around 8.30pm.

Stefan to the group

Hi all, Orlagh Woods from the New Work Network is looking into the possibility of us doing a performance of 'Song Books' at a 'Late at Tate' in the autumn. If the Tate go for this then she will make an application for funding, so we could each get a small fee.

I'm not sure how likely this is to come off, but thought I'd let you know in case you have any views. I made it clear that you'd have to agree and the Tate is being approached with that caveat. If that doesn't happen, there is also the possibility of doing it at the Toynbee Studios - a very nice intimate theatre space with an enormous stage in Aldgate.

Hope to see some of you this Saturday at the Cardew concert in Conway Hall. I'm not sure if I can get there early. Carolyn has suggested meeting at 12.30 or 1pm. Please contact her if you can do that.

Jane Alden to Stefan

I am honoured that you want me to participate in Song Books on March 11. I look forward to being in touch with you and the others about how I should prepare (which songs, etc.).

I have booked my flight from the USA now. Getting in Saturday evening, so should be ready to rehearse at 2pm on Sunday afternoon.

I went to the Eddie Prévost launch at Cafe Oto this evening. Nice acoustic.

Looking forward to it!

Stefan to Jane

Hi Jane, Great to meet you at Conway Hall yesterday. First of all, apologies for not completing our previous communication properly. I'm glad to hear that your production of Cardew's 'Treatise' at Morley College went so well.

It would be really exciting to have you jet in to take part in our Song Books performance at Cafe Oto on the 11th March! We will be there all afternoon from about 2pm, for a 7.30pm start. So there is time to try the acoustics out, warm up, meet the others and so on. When you confirm you want to do this, I will circulate an email announcement to the rest of the participants and you can communicate with them directly if you want to.

We've been meeting to get to know each other and discuss issues relating to the score, and for individuals to choose which songs to trial. In terms of background study, I'm particularly keen that people think about the space between Satie and Thoreau. We can read scores in performance, and perhaps even show which score we are performing at any time with a visible number.

I'm attaching our draft press release in which I've included your name - let me know if you decide you can't do it.

Have a good mid-winter break.

Ali Warner to the group

I go to [Eddie Prevost's Improvisation] Workshop about once a season, and last time I was there I saw Grundik. He is keen to offer electronics in the performance, and would like a defined next step of how he can be involved - he was sorry he couldn't be at the last rehearsal. We discussed having a trio rehearsal with him - Geri and I - which he was interested in, so I can set that up.

Chapter 1 Section 3

Song Books 1 – Cafe Oto

PRESS RELEASE

Performance of 'Song Books' by John Cage

7.30pm 11th March 2012 at Cafe Oto

18-22 Ashwin street, Dalston

London, E8 3DL

Scratch Orchestra members disembowel Cage's magnum opus, with a sharp younger generation of performers as their accomplices.

Description of the score

This is one of Cage's most ambitious works. It comprises over 48 actual songs, and 42 instructions for 'theatre' (Fluxus-like 'actions' for the most part), which are performed using random starting times within a set period. The scores are very diverse and cover almost every approach to experimenting with notation that Cage used, from conventional music to the most abstract. The libretto is also very varied and covers most of Cage's interests, from mushrooms to anarchy. Each 'song' is designated to be either with or without electronics. Performers of songs are asked to be cognisant of 'the space between Satie and Thoreau', or not, which I think defines Cage's notion of the avant-garde in a nutshell.

Intention of the project

To raise the question of the place of visual performance within experimental musics. The older core performers were in the Scratch Orchestra which was deeply imbued with a visual dimension going back to Cardew's earlier composition 'Treatise', and brought to the fore in Scratch performances by the activities of the Slippery Merchants.

It is also an attempt to bring Scratch experience into a critical collision with a contemporaneous John Cage, in collaboration with a younger generation of performers and composers. John Tilbury: *"Cage achieved mythical status, but Cardew was a legend"*.

Performers to include: Stefan Szczelkun, Peter Ellison, Carole Finer, Linn D, Michael Parsons (all above ex-Scratch Orchestra), Eve Libertine, Geri McEwan, Ali Warner, Renate Biruls, Portia Winters, Robbie Lockwood, Lucy Galland, Tom Mudd, Jane Alden from USA, Simon Walton, and electronics by Grundik Kasyansky.

The first performance happens and is a sell-out success, with people queuing around the block.

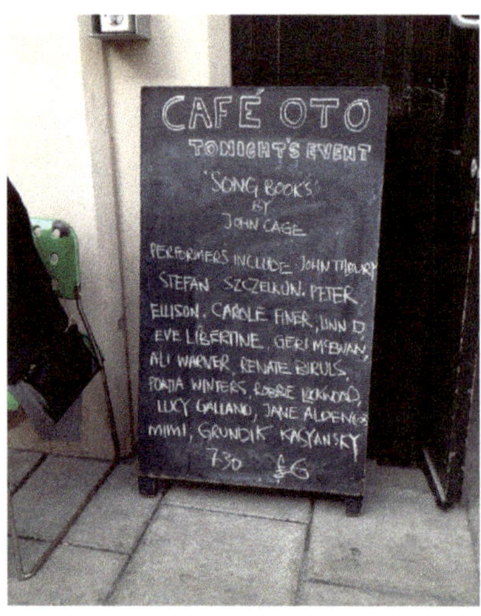

Review of 'Song Books' Ben Harper (12 March 2012)

Boring Like A Drill Blog

It must be about dead-on a year ago that I first saw a performance of John Cage's vast, protean Song Books. That time it was Exaudi at King's Place. Last night I got to experience it again, enacted by a hodge-podge of players including a bunch of old Scratch Orchestra alumni, at Cafe Oto. On the surface, the approaches taken by the two groups were broadly similar, but it was through the details that the work can truly live or die.

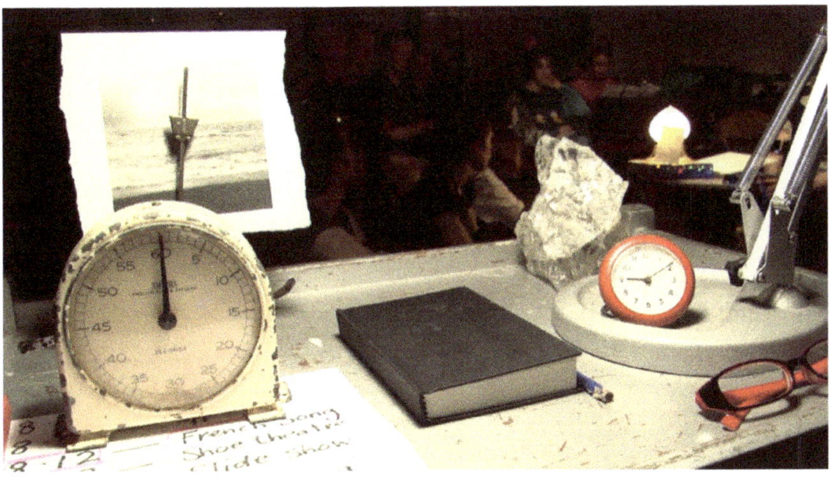

I almost didn't get to see it this time. I hadn't booked a ticket and when I got there a queue was already stretching down the street and around the corner. The place was rammed: the crowded atmosphere emphasised by having punters sitting in amongst the performers in the 'stage' area, and other performers scattered in amongst the standing crowd. Exaudi had a similar setup of their singers stationed around the audience, moving from one spot to the next from time to time. The crowd at King's Place, however, remained seated in the middle throughout. Besides the milling crowd at Oto, there was also the bar and pavement outside luring punters in and out for refreshment.

On both nights, the programme was set up to last an hour, in the space of which each player independently performed a chance-determined programme of solos from the Books. Exaudi played their pieces expertly – I want to say impeccably. It was a faithful, thoughtful interpretation of Cage's music, but it felt remote and clinical. It was 'art', mounted and framed. With the Scratch Orchestra et al., things were more chaotic, a little rougher round the edges but no less faithful in interpretation. Some players were a little too enthusiastic, swatting at tables with paper plates or menacing punters with alligator masks. Others were a little too reticent, like the couple who spent most of the time in the centre of the room, singing in unison, apparently more to themselves than to the audience.

It was precisely this diversity that made last night at Oto the more rewarding experience, as we all saw and participated in an enactment of Cage's aesthetic and social values of the time: of diversity, abundance, coexistence, anarchy, the merging of art and life. For an hour or so everyone in the bar experienced Cage's vision for the world in microcosm. The crowded room inevitably cramped some of the theatrical elements called for in the score, but compromises were made, punters made room as necessary. In other words, there was true, unselfconscious audience interaction and participation, without coercion.

In this atmosphere, the chance coincidences and juxtapositions took on more than just an aesthetic appeal. At one point a pretty lady in a red dress stood and repeatedly intoned Thoreau's anarchist maxim "The best form of government is no government." Behind her, a pianist began playing Cage's lovely 1949 composition Dream. Soon after this was almost drowned out by insistent hammering. All three carried on unperturbed. When the hour was up, this same woman in red had just been tasked with typing out a phrase of Erik Satie's, 38 times, on a recalcitrant manual typewriter. The audience stood around intently, and waited patiently in silence until she was finally done.

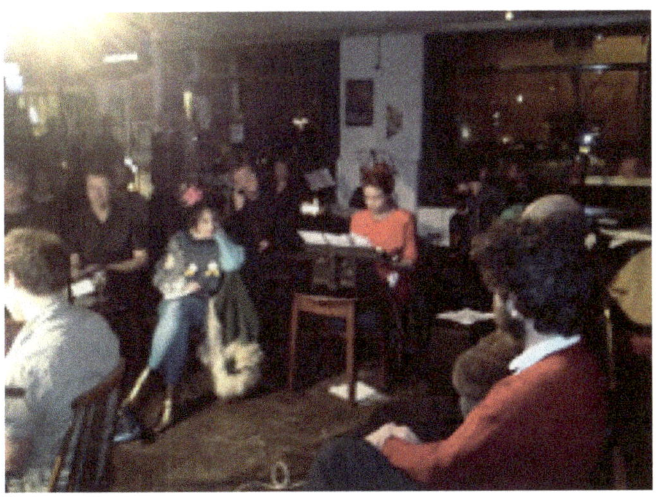

The Oto performance succeeded as art because so much more of life was able to infiltrate it. Whenever I think I understand Cage a little better, a new complication appears. I keep thinking of Morton Feldman's challenge, "Is music an artform? Or is it just showbiz?" (For this argument, the Exaudi gig was showbiz.) Cage's music is definitely art and yet, in this case at least, the closer it comes to life the better it works as art. Put that way, Cage sounds like an old-fashioned mimetic artist, but what he achieves is not mimicry of life, rather he recreates certain principles on which life conducts itself. What bugs me about this is: if interpretation of Cage's work were to continue to approach 'real life' closer and closer, at some point it would cease to be art. If we accept Cage's conceit that there is no distinction between life and art, life may be permitted to intrude upon a performance of Cage to the extent that it misrepresents Cage's work. There is some undefined tipping point within Cage's work whereupon it refutes itself.

Therefore, to be like life, Cage's music must always remain as art, to some extent. Of course, there is a distinction between art, as witnessed at Cafe Oto, and artifice.

Geri McEwan's prolonged typing solo finally ends!

Chapter 1 Section 4

Song Books 2 - Toynbee Studios Theatre

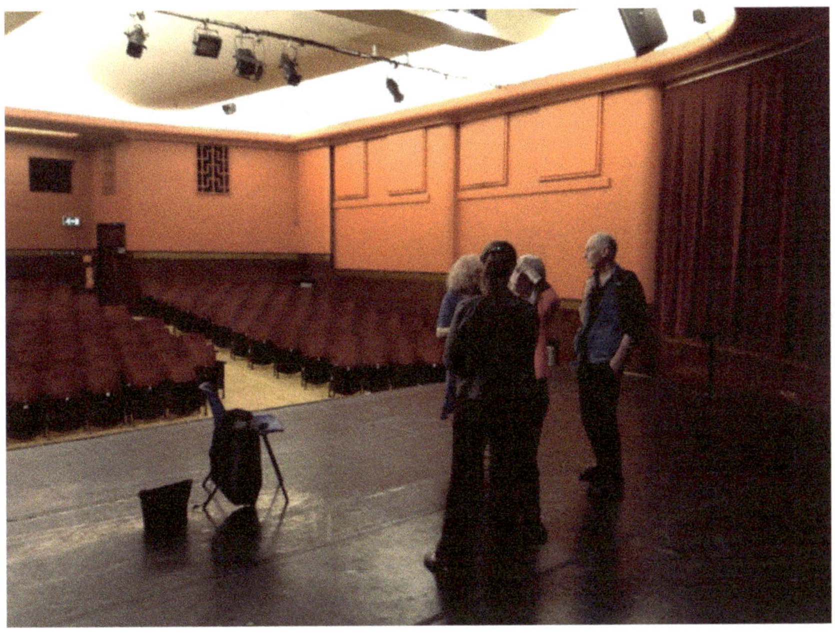

Visiting Toynbee Theatre before the performance - Carole, Jane, Linn, Michael.

Stefan to group

Our next performance is now booked for Saturday 20 October 2012, starting at 8pm. Toynbee Studios Theatre is an art deco theatre which retains many of its original features, including 280 fixed seats and a larger-than-average stage that could have 50 performers on it. The performance will be promoted by Artsadmin and the New Work Network (NWN). Orlagh Woods of NWN has been negotiating with Gill and Jessica at Artsadmin. The ticket price of £6 for concessions and £7 for everyone else is fine by me. They have to pay several staff.

We need to sort the publicity text (150 words) plus image for Friday. We can view the theatre during the week of July 9th, following our meeting at Oto on the 8th.

Stefan to group (29 June 2012)

I suggest we need just two meetings before the event. One soon to assess the last performance and think about what changes we'd like to make. And a second a week or two before the actual performance. Sub-groups are welcome to have more meetings of course. How about Sunday 8th July at Cafe Oto from 2pm for the earlier one? Then we can arrange the time and place of a pre-performance meeting then.

I'm hoping to arrange a Scratch Orchestra study/performance project following on from this performance.

Carolyn to group

Greetings Stefan. I would very much like to do the same Songs, but as I missed several of the lead-up meetings [for the last performance], I learnt – last week – that people did 3 songs whereas I did 5 (so sorry). I chose mostly theatre/action pieces with not much sound, so in one sense I was not overloading the aural ambience. But I realise this is tricky. If you would like me to do 3, of course I will. Others might like to do the vocal pieces/sound pieces they did before, but also pop in a less vocal theatre piece as well if it would fit? I wait to hear from you.

PRESS RELEASE

'Song Books' by John Cage at Toynbee Studios Theatre

An Artsadmin programme

"... to consider the Song Books as a work of art is nearly impossible. Who would dare? It resembles a brothel, doesn't it?" John Cage

Saturday 20th October 2012

8–9pm; Bar from 7pm

Tickets: £7/£6 concessions/New Work Network members

New Work Network presents John Cage's 'Songbooks' performed by ex-Scratch Orchestra members alongside a younger generation of performers and composers.

Fresh from their sell-out concert at Cafe Oto, the group perform one of Cage's most ambitious works, comprising over 48 vocal scores and 42 other instructions for 'theatre' (Fluxus-like 'actions' for the most part), individually programmed by each performer to start within an agreed period of time. The scores are diverse and cover almost every approach to experimenting with notation that Cage used, from conventional music to the most abstract.

The piece raises the question of the place of visual performance within experimental music, and attempts to bring the Scratch Orchestra experience into a critical collision with a John Cage composition.

Performers include: Renate Biruls, Linn D, Carole Finer, Lucie Galand, Grundik Kasyansky, Eve Libertine, Robbie Lockwood, Geri McEwan, Michael Parsons, Stefan Szczelkun, Sarah Walker, Simon Walton, Ali Warner and Portia Winters.

"Cage's music is definitely art and yet, in this case at least, the closer it comes to life the better it works as art." Ben Harper, Boring Like A Drill, 12 March 2012

The performance at Toynbee happened as planned, and went well. It was not a sell-out as with the previous performance at Oto but was well attended and covered the quite high overheads.

Stefan to group (26 October 2012)

Hi Everyone,

Here are the accounts of our Song Books concert at Toynbee Theatre. The balance after expenses was £266.38, of which Artsadmin gets £106.55 (40%) and NWN £159.83 (60%) as agreed in our contract. Orlagh of NWN agreed to reduce their costs from £150 to £100. So, we will get £59.93.

What shall we do with this? Thirteen performers on the night. £4.61 each or we could pay it to Bryn as a fee for the recording. Thinking about this, I think that's what I'd recommend.

It looks like there will be a review in The Wire by Phil England!

Toynbee Performance: Recording and Review

Stefan's email to the group about the recording

The broadcast of Bryn Harris's recording of our 'Song Books' will be on Resonance Radio on Boxing Day, with a programme beginning at 5pm. Resonance 104.4 FM if you are in London, or online if you are not. This will start with Carol's previously recorded show about

‘Song Books’ made with Penny Homer, as an introduction. Then the recording of ‘Song Books’ at Toynbee Theatre will be played. The remaining part of the programme up to 7pm might be me reading

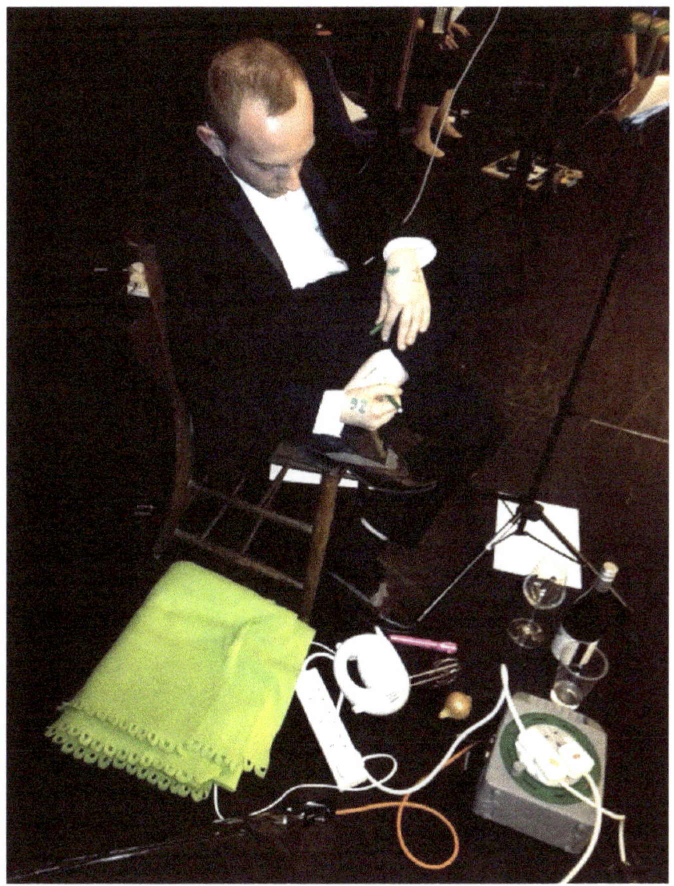

George Chambers making his preparations

from Nature Study Notes, as a way of leading from Cage to the proposed new project.

Review of 'Song Books' Phil England (February 2013)

The Wire #348

The lights dim in this red velvet art deco theatre and we are plunged into darkness. The players have determined that they will each have their own personal lighting arrangement and only be illuminated while they are performing. Very quickly two or three performers start playing overlapping selections from Song Books – a collection of around 90 solo pieces either for voice or theatre, some of which have instructions for electronic treatments.

Former Scratch Orchestra member Stefan Szczelkun has assembled a dozen or so former colleagues and younger players for the evening - a follow-up to their packed-out production at Cafe Oto back in March. For this performance, the group has agreed that each member will prepare and enact three "songs" each over the course of an hour, with start points predetermined independently in advance.

Initially a sense of whimsy and the juvenile pervades. One person is climbing through and over the audience, another is playing music from Cage's Suite for Toy Piano and a silhouetted Szczelkun is galloping back and forth slapping his thigh. For a while it all feels very 1960s Scratch Orchestra but displaced into an entirely different social and cultural context.

Is this going to be a lightweight snook? Cage treated as mere avant-garde jester? Has the flexibility of interpretation that Cage affords in this 1970 composition been abused and not balanced with a requisite amount of responsibility to the aesthetic potential of the work?

Partly this is the wrong question. Acts of theatre make up about half of the "songs" and unlike most of Cage's work, Song

Books is designed to allow the performer's personality and subjectivity to come through via the process of selection and interpretation. And as the sixty minutes unfold we are forced to shed our likes and dislikes and adjust to the rich variety of juxtapositions as the natural order of things. It is this balance of freedom, responsibility and acceptance that is the necessary precondition for the anarchist society that Cage's aesthetic aims to prepare the ground for.

The fine group of female singers - Eve Libertine, Sharon Gal, Portia Winters, Ali Warner and Penny Homer - take the challenge of Cage's unconventional notation with an appropriate seriousness. The piece ebbs and flows so that it's sometimes dense, sometimes sparse; the balance of theatre and vocal pieces shifts around; and occasionally some delightful groupings of vocal works fall together in accidental harmony and unintended conversation.

In one of Libertine's performances the former Crass vocalist ends up interacting - in a confidently negotiated taut vocal tightrope - with two recordings of herself. When tenor George Chambers sings a list of random celebrity names to the tune of "Rule, Britannia!", the collision of cultural resonances combines to hilarious effect. The piece ends with a fragile operatic rendering of the Henry Thoreau text which provides the work's underlying theme: "That government is best which governs not at all; and when men are prepared for it, that will be the kind of government which they will have."

Some Afterthoughts from performers and audience members

Stefan Szczelkun: What the singers might not have seen was the use of light projected onto the back wall of the stage, that I hope gave depth to the visuality of the concert depth. I projected four slides re. Thoreau (of plotland chalets), did a shadow dance and used an overhead projector in a subtle way. I also looked at the audience through a magnifier sheet whilst holding a micro torch to my mouth, hopefully creating an eerie effect. Carolyn was dancing into rear stage with glow sticks and with fairy lights.

When I came to give my apple to the audience, the guy in the seat I had designated was sound asleep. I knelt next to him and ever so gently woke him up. "So Sorry to wake you! But here is an apple from my garden." He seemed to be happy, if (albeit) sleepy!

Later reading a book at front stage, I had the title of the book 'Last of the Hippies' running across my iPhone and used my micro torch to read. So, there was subtle lighting happening. At another time when I stormed out the door only to return with a scary crocodile head on, I wanted it to be gloomy to be more scary and dreamlike. So that was me and what I remember of my lighting!!

Bron Jones: I didn't see a lot as I didn't want to be looking around, favouring the calm looking-forward stance when not performing! I sometimes saw things happening in front of me. Carol - typing like she was at home with the lamp on. I saw Portia's light going on and off beneath me. Stefan – running up the aisle with a beaky mask on, looking quite threateningly at the audience. Ali's first song, which I liked a lot, and so did look round a bit and liked the stillness of the performance. Renate – doing the 'I can take my shoes off' theatre instruction over the other side. Carolyn – being very active and getting cross with bubbles and balls in front stage; bubbles not working and then balls being dropped and rolling away. Calm, altar-like toy piano with coloured candles lower centre stage played by concert pianist looking the part! [Sarah Walker - the Radio 3 presenter]

[Bron then writes about what Songs she performed:]

* I gave a bunch of grapes (large cranberries) to a designated seat which was empty between two people. I said 'this is for you' to the seat.

* Solo for voice 33. Using two tape recorders. First to sing French words by Satie at various speeds then sing with the recording, and record then play both together. (A racket!)

* Solo for voice 86. Slide show on computer, moving to three angles so all of the audience could see.

* Solo for voice 3 with electronics. Sing words about a hawk, whilst going down a river in Concord, Massachusetts i.e. using a map of a river as a graphic score and leaving the boat and walking to the house at the top. Playing hawk sounds.

* Solo for voice 5 with electronics. Thoreau's portrait, life-size, on both sides of a card held up in front of my face. I sang the word fragments given using the lines that made up the features of Thoreau's face as a graphic score, and played a recording of weather (strong wind), changing the volume.

* Prepare food. Grated carrot, cut bread and cucumber, and made a sandwich with all those things and hummus.

Ali Warner: I thought Renate's torch down her cleavage pointing upwards worked well (and also George's torch pointing upwards in his top pocket), but I couldn't see Carmel, for example, as her bike light was weak/flashing and wasn't directed on her! Was everyone's lighting strong enough? [We had agreed to use only 'personal lighting', which meant none of the stage lighting was used.]

Stefan: I've just listened to Bryn Harris's recording of our 'Song Books'. There are many lovely moments. The main structure is provided by Carol's old typewriter that hammers away from 21:40 minutes in duration from the start of the performance to 46:46. It evokes the mechanisation of the literary world, that now sounds so anachronistic. It is a reminder of the domination of music that was attempted by the classical humanist tradition - with its [gradually standardised] published scores. Cage was both part of that, and squirming against it. There is a great moment when a woman is shush-shushing, and then the typewriter finally stops. Is that all it takes?

Sally Labern [in the audience]

What I loved was the context of the demo, subtly woven into the work. [The theatre was decorated with posters of a recent anti austerity march]

Emilyn Claid [in the audience]

Stefan, I never got to tell you how very moved I felt by the performance of John Cage's work at Toynbee Hall. Seeing you perform again after all these years was just great, and the piece took me back to another time, another life. Thank you...and your skipping dance was delightful!

Chapter 2

Cornelius Cardew's Scratch Orchestra

'Nature Study Notes' Orchestral improvisation, Organisation and Process

The improvisation rites, collected by Cornelius Cardew as 'Nature Study Notes', were written by many people who attended the Experimental Music classes at Morley College taught by Cardew, Michael Parsons and Howard Skempton in 1969. The collection from that time comprises 152 written rites. These were collated, hand-written and printed by Cornelius Cardew. A copy of this beautiful publication was given to each person who joined the Scratch Orchestra. Some rites were instructions for performance and others were 'rites' that set the tone for an improvisation.

It was this collection that was the foundational text of the Scratch Orchestra, along with 'Scratch Music'. In the founding constitution, a Scratch Orchestra was defined as: "A large number of enthusiasts pooling their resources (not primarily material resources) and assembling for action (music-making, performance, edification)." (The Musical Times, June 1969).

It was decided to introduce these improvisation rites to a younger generation of performers, both for historical interest and to see if they still 'worked', forty years later. Many of the core group from the exploration into John Cage's 'Song Books' continued on to the Nature Study Notes project.

There was an improvement on one copy of the Song Books score I had bought and the subsequent photocopies that performers had to work with. This time I had printed facsimiles of the original 'Nature Study Notes' booklet and everyone had one.

Nature Study Notes: Introduction

"Draw a straight line and follow it." (LaMonte Young, 1960)

As I have written above, the rites were collected from the Experimental Music class that Cornelius and colleagues taught on Friday evening at Morley College from the autumn of 1968 (Tilbury, 2008). This included visual artists, as well as student musicians who had been studying under Cardew at the Royal Academy of Music.

"The collection of 'Nature Study Notes' was started at the Morley College class, I think early in 1969. This should not be described as a composition class; the Experimental Music class was run by

Cornelius. I joined as a student in November 1968. I think Cor launched the idea of Nature Study Notes to encourage everyone to contribute to a collection of inspirational texts, to be used as starting points for collective playing together so that everyone would feel equally involved; and as an alternative to composition directed by individual members (although this was encouraged as well). (It might be worth also checking with Chris Hobbs and Hugh Shrapnel, who were among the first contributors to the collection)." (Michael Parsons, 2016, by email)

At the start of the booklet, Cardew states that: "No rights are reserved on the book of rites. They may be reproduced and performed freely." Cardew extends an open invitation to people to contribute to a second set and in the draft constitution Cardew states; "Members should constantly bear in mind the possibility of contributing new rites." A 'rite' is defined in the draft constitution as different to a composition:

"An improvisation rite is not a musical composition; it does not attempt to influence the music that will be played; at most it may establish a community of feeling, or a communal starting point, through ritual." (Draft Constitution, 1969)

Indeed, "Psi Ellison went so far as to regard them as the regeneration, renewal and development of an urban folk art." (Tilbury, 2008) And finally, John Tilbury also writes that; "Perhaps more than any other category, the Improvisation Rites characterised the essential nature of the orchestra."

The rites are listed in the booklet in order of collection. The first rite is by Howard Skempton, HSDN01. "Any number of drums. Introduction of the pulse. Continuation of the pulse. Deviation through emphasis, decoration, contradiction."

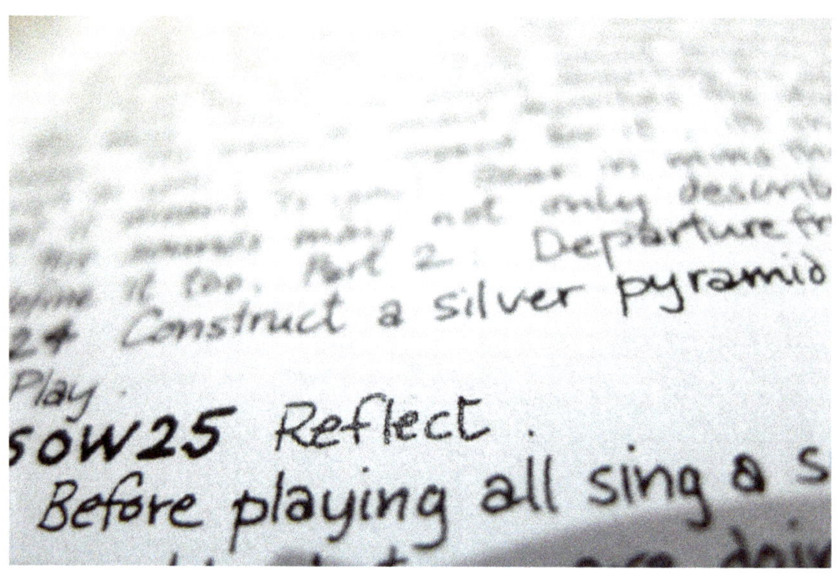

Photos above by Emmanuelle Waeckerle

This rite, known as 'Drum Number 1', defines a ground zero of improvisation at the time the Scratch Orchestra was formed. A group agreement or starting point is developed by way of the fundamental dimensions of 'emphasis, decoration and contradiction'.

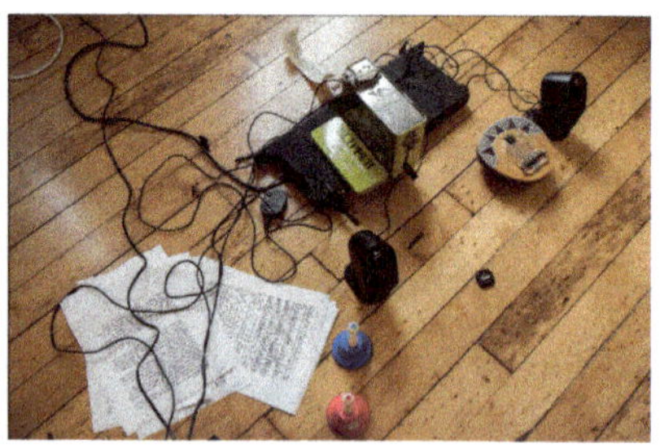

Photograph by Martin Dixon

Another very basic and open description of improvisation is then given five rites further down, in Hugh Shrapnel's first rite, HMSIR5,

HSDNO 1 Any number of drums. Introduction of the pulse. Continuation of the pulse. Deviation through emphasis, decoration, contradiction.

CCIR 2 Initiate an improvisation in the following way: All seated loosely in a circle, each player shall write or draw on each of the ten fingernails of the player on his left. No action or sound is to be made by a player after his fingernails have received this writing or drawing other than music.
Closing rite: each player shall erase the marks from the fingernails of another player. Your participation in the music ceases when the marks have been erased from your fingernails.

PDIR 3 Form a standing circle. Nominate a leader, who stands in centre with eye's blindfolded. The remainder of group rotate slowly around him/her. At random the leader indicates a quarter of the group number by touching each individual. Indicated ones leave the group and become 'outers'.
The leader removes his blindfold, and establishes a rhythm and a note of his choice. The group together sing the note, which once established may be enlarged upon freely; but with voice only.
At any time during above proceeding an 'outer' may touch one of 'inner' group, who must immediately cease part in the performance and assume role of non-participating 'outer'. 'Outer' automatically becomes an 'inner' and must begin to perform a new sound or activity. One not produced by the voice.
Thus an outer may terminate any one person's participation at any time.
When the leader is touched, he forfeits his role and so doing shouts 'Porridge'. All activities and sounds must cease immediately, whereupon the new leader is blindfolded and rite begins anew. The new leader must decide upon a new group activity once 'outers' have been re-indicated. No verbal instruction must be given. He must begin the performance, the group imitate and enlarge upon it.
Each successive rite must follow the same ritualistic pattern.

FRMEVR 4 Each person entering performance space receives a number in order. Anyone can give an order (imperatively obeyable) to a higher number, and must obey orders given him by a lower number. No 1 receives his orders from the current highest number (the most recently entered player); the highest number can give orders only to No 1.

✓ **HMSIR 5** For any number of people, preferably unknown to each other, making any kind of vocal or physical sound; no instruments to be used.
Performance to take place in any large area, inside or outside, with everyone scattered throughout whole areas, widely separated from each other as possible. A person stays in the same place throughout the performance; physical motion of all kind to be kept to a minimum.
Sounds can be of any kind produced from the person, ie. vocal sounds (singing, speaking, whispering, shouting, crying, laughing, hissing, etc) or from the body (hissing, slapping, clapping, etc).
Sounds are made mainly in response to other sounds, therefore a sound made should have some meaning to the person making it. This meaning can be verbal (conversational) or aural (musical), or a combination of both. A response can be immediate (spontaneous reaction to some kind of sound, probably verbal) or reflective (probably musical). He can also arouse the response of other people by some sound, or he can just listen. In general the nature of the improvisation should be still and reflective.
The performance ends for each person individually when he has nothing more he wants to do. He may then get up and leave, this being the only physical movement he makes.

FRFRR 6 Announce a collective improvisation in which anyone can take part. The announcement should be accompanied by the following text:
"Look around and let yourself be drawn to a person whom you like. Study his face, gestures, movements for a while. Then take a sum of money, preferably all you have in your pocket, and give it to him. Then start again."
Musicians attempt to be more likeable than the general public. It is not important whether or no money is actually raised. End is open.

✓ **CCSBR 7** Take a stupid book. A reader reads aloud from it while the rest improvise. The role of reader may wander, a) through the reader presenting the stupid book to someone else, and b) by someone wresting the stupid book from the reader. A reader may attempt to terminate proceedings by ceasing to read aloud from the stupid book.

HSIR 8 The group assembles, one of the members being elected BIG LEADER. When there is silence, the BIG LEADER makes a sound, as short and quiet as possible. He is then challenged, the challenging member attempting to produce a sound even shorter and more quiet than the first. In the midst of great celebration, the challenger becomes BIG LEADER. The process then continues until all members have had a chance of becoming BIG LEADER. The challenger who last becomes BIG LEADER is named as the SUPER BIG LEADER. There is great celebration, drinking, music, &c.

✓ **MC 9** 17 people play simultaneously at one piano.

MC 10 Wash.

MC 11 Measure length, breadth and height of room of performance, taking account of any consistent prominences. Use the figures in any way to organise sounds.

MC 12 Two classes of performers: improvisers and stone-throwers, the former class to contain more members than the latter.
The stone throwers throw stones to miss the improvisers and cause no damage, with a vigour proportionate to the intensity of the sound.

HSIRNT 13 When you're not playing, look for a girl in red stockings.

HSIRNT 14 Before playing, do something inappropriate. Keep doing it until it seems inappropriate to start playing. Start playing. [15 and 15A overleaf]

✓ **CCPR 16** Within a certain overall playing-time each player determines by random means one or more stretches during which he will play, for the rest remaining silent.
Players with access to mechanical or electrical equipment may make 2 parts, one of which would be performed by the mechanical or electrical equipment, the player simply switching it on and off at the appropriate points.

CCAR 17 At a signal all players commence playing a continuous accompaniment. As the spirit moves them, individual players rise and play solos. After soloing, rest. After resting, play more accompaniment (the same as before or different). Cease playing at a signal.
Definition: An accompaniment is music that allows a solo – in the event of one being played – to be appreciated as such.

JH

3

entitled 'Improvisation Rite': "Any number of people making any sounds. Perform in a large area, as widely separated from each other as possible. Performers stay in the same place throughout, keeping physical movement to a minimum.' (This is the more compact description given in the notes on this rite at the back of the booklet.) It then goes on to demand that 'a sound should have some meaning to the person making it' and that the performer 'can just listen'. The direction is to be reflective rather than play willy-nilly. A later rite by Cardew (CCIRTSOW25) simply instructs us to 'Reflect'.

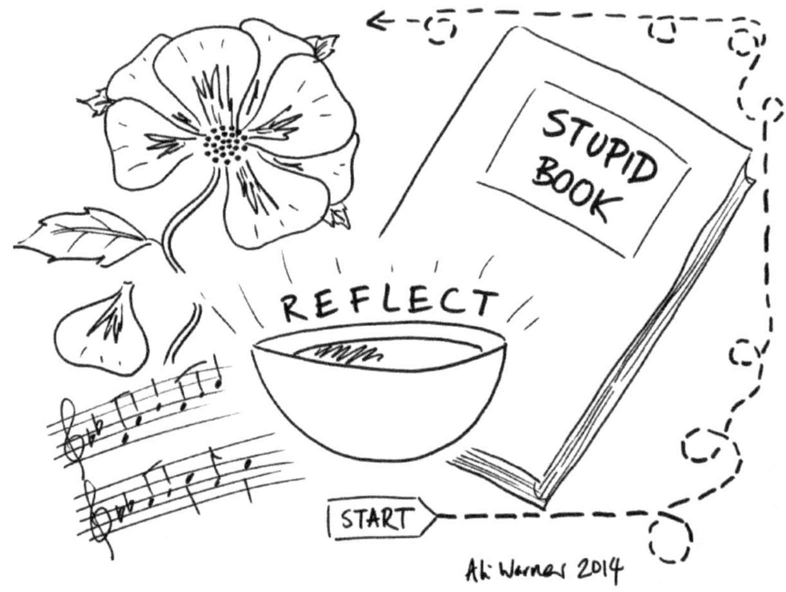

Cornelius Cardew's rites take a poetic approach that has the stamp of his authorship. For instance, CCSBR7 states: "Take a stupid book. A reader reads aloud from it while the rest improvise. The role of reader may wander, a) through the reader presenting the stupid book to someone else, and b) by someone wrestling the stupid book from the reader. A reader may attempt to terminate proceedings by ceasing to read aloud from the stupid book." In the rite notes,

Cardew suggests more drastic actions may be needed: "To end, stronger measures may be necessary, e.g. Destruction of the S.B." This rite was popular in the group and was performed by Carol Finer, with a feminist twist, in both the concerts discussed below.

Here's another basic rite by Phillip Dadson, the 'Passing Time' rite or PDTR30: "Pass time. If passing time bores you, pause to listen. If listening to time passing bores you, invent a distraction to pass time by." This implies that performers should not bring material to the performance. They wait, if necessary, for it to arise within the performance time.

Some such rites seem designed to go against what might be considered the pitfalls of free improvisation, such as egocentric attention-seeking or a person playing loudly without listening. Generally, the idea of improvising 'accompaniments' is encouraged: "An accompaniment is defined as music that allows a solo (in the event of one occurring) to be appreciated as such." (Draft Constitution, 1969)

Conventional tunes may be included. See Bryn Harris' BHWSR35: "Think of a score and play it. If you can't think of one augment someone else's playing."

Lightness and irreverence is valued. "Before improvisation, tell a few jokes to get everyone into a good humour." That is HSSR52 by Howard Skempton. But also, occasionally, darker psychodrama is invited: "Those present, hiss nonchalantly to themselves. The assembly undergoes slow metamorphosis – to a snarling mob, pulling hideous faces at each other. Proceed from here into some other activity." That is David Jackman with his rite DJ68.

For some reason, not many women published rites in the original edition of 'Nature Study Notes'. Women were a minority in the Scratch Orchestra overall, and even those that were members seem to have contributed less written material than their male counterparts. What a difference from then to now, however, with women as the majority of members and contributors in recent projects. Original Scratch member, Carol Finer, came up with one of the most political rites with her CFIRT146: "Page one of the Evening Standard current on the day of the performance. Each performer will have a copy, which he will use as his score. Performers decide individually how they wish to interpret the score and perform accordingly for a given length of time." Carol had been using newspapers as a starting point in her work with students at Camberwell College of Art.

https://soundcloud.com/szczels/nature-study-notes-16mins

Stefan to the group (4 July 2014)

"Music-making is a participatory group activity that serves to unite black people into a cohesive group for a common purpose."(Portia K. Maultsby, 1991, p.187, as quoted by Everard M. Phillips, member of the audience for the 'Nature Study Notes' performance at Chisenhale, from his 2009 book, 'The Political Calypso'.)

Of course, this unification through music-making goes for all people, and it seems to have acted on us via the Chisenhale performance. The desire to meet up, expressed in all the emails, was surely a result of the group 'cohesion' that had arisen from the previous music-making, and the desire to talk was perhaps to find a 'common purpose'. Whatever that might mean, it has a strong political ring to it. Maybe our dispersion geographically (and in other ways) means that it's not easy to come together and 'find' this common purpose? Is this an endemic problem of modern art culture, ever since it became alienated from community and individualised?

Does the process of preparing for a performance of Scratch Music produce the desire for a 'common purpose', which then finds expression in discussion afterwards? Or is Scratch Music a catalyst for the emergence of a 'common purpose' or collective being, in the way that music is capable of expressing otherwise inchoate desires?

I think there is no single answer to this question. A few of the rites in 'Nature Study Notes' allow direct articulation of dissent, like the 'Stupid Book' rite. Should more? Most in the booklet simply allow us to feel a unity of expression that transcends our diversity and anti-social tendencies. Beautiful moments of music give us an insight into the power and wonder of our 'general intellect' (Marx, 1858).

Although the rites seem to be a unique and extraordinary collective achievement of the Sixties which are still able to channel relevant contemporary action, we should nonetheless think of ways that we could all make rites for today. I've hinted above at the importance of the 'Stupid Book' rite, and there are others like Carol Finer's rite using newspaper front pages that I also mentioned. Could there be more like that? What is the 'bee in your bonnet' that could do with a ritual to give it concrete expression?

Improvisation does model a human capacity to find joint enterprise, simply by being together to meet a common purpose. But even if this is the case, do we not need to think about how this creative situation could fuse with more widely spread cultural processes and human needs?

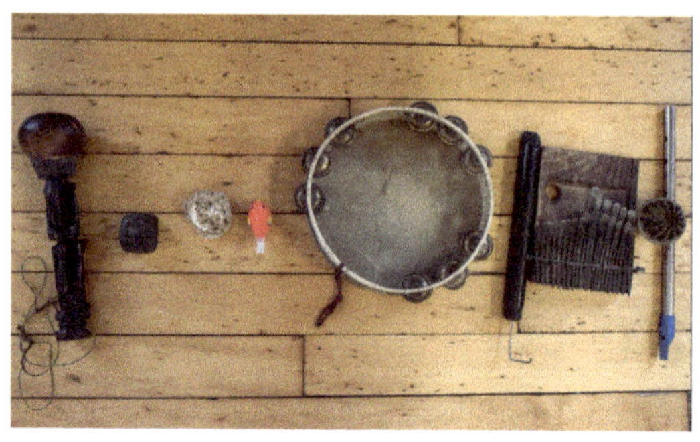

Photograph by Martin Dixon

Nature Study Notes: Organisation and Process

Stefan to Tony Burch (20 October 2013)

Tony, nice to meet you at the X6 seminar at Chisenhale on Sunday. [X6 was a dance collective in the late Seventies, with a famous dance space in Butlers Wharf just south of Tower Bridge.] Emilyn gave me your email, and I hope you don't mind me contacting you. Really, I'd like your advice as to how to go about moving forward the idea of a Scratch Orchestra intergenerational event at Chisenhale Dance Space. The project would follow up on the success of the John Cage's 'Song Books' events I organised in 2011 & 2012. The performances, at Cafe Oto and Artsadmin's Theatre at Toynbee Hall, involved some original Scratch Orchestra people as well as a younger generation of singers. They were an acclaimed success with a review in *The Wire*. My idea this time is to base the work on a collection of Fluxus-like short instructions, that are published in a booklet under the title of 'Nature Study Notes'. It was these improvisation rites that fired and inspired the early phase of the Scratch Orchestra (1969). The pre-performance workshops could be open to Chisenhale dancers and performers. I think the Chisenhale space would work very well for this sort of performance. Do you think this might interest the Chisenhale management group? If so, please advise on the best approach!

The negotiation that ensued resulted in a booking at Chisenhale finally being confirmed for June 2014. Social media had really taken-off by 2014, so creating an Event on Facebook for performances had become an important part of our organising and exchanging of ideas. Chisenhale Dance Space is in East London, and has the original tea warehouse floor brought from the X6 Dance Space in Butlers Wharf.

Stefan to Carole, Ali, Bron and Michael Parsons (4 November 2013)

Hi, hope this finds you well. I was thinking of proceeding with the idea of exploring 'Nature Study Notes' and beyond in 2014, with a performance at Chisenhale Dance Space. With its flat dance floor and warehouse aesthetic, I think it has a good atmosphere. It costs only £180 for a basic package and I have that in the bank. It could include new performers that frequent Chisenhale. But could people get there easily, and could we attract a music audience to a space they are not used to?

I could also ask at Oto, where we are more likely to get an audience and would probably cover costs again. Might work well in parallel with Chisenhale? If you are into this but not available for parts of 2014, please let me know your availability. I was thinking of after Easter sometime.

Ali Warner to Stefan (November 2013)

Dear Stefan, thank you for involving me in this next stage of our potential explorations – you/our group have been coming up in my mind for some time, and I was wondering what could happen next.

I'm keen to be part of taking this further. I don't have any time specifically unavailable in 2014 yet, and I would like to give time to this.

I think there's something in your instinct around the Chisenhale space that is worth following – and your idea to involve Chisenhale performers is a good one, particularly in terms of making connections to that area and potential audiences. Yes, it could be good to do something at Cafe Oto too – but Chisenhale is where my energy is going first. It's not so far out of central London, is it?

I do think part of the draw [for the audience] at Cafe Oto/ Toynbee was John Cage, so it's also worth considering anything further we might need to do in terms of communications to inspire an audience that might be less familiar with the Scratch Orchestra (although it's still well-known in experimental music & art circles, I'm sure).

Stefan to the group (8 March 2014)

There are about eight good people that have so far variously confirmed that they will be able to do the performance of selections from 'Nature Study Notes' on June 28th at Chisenhale Dance Space. The pre-performance meetings will involve reading 'Nature Study Notes' together and discussing scores that people are intrigued by. Later, we will discuss how to structure the performance at Chisenhale Dance Space using these scores. Meetings can have a limited number of carefully chosen guests.

Let us meet on Sunday 23rd March 2pm to (no later than) 4pm in Cafe Oto. At that meeting, we will arrange a mid-week meeting that is convenient for Sharon who works on Sundays. The next meeting, at which the structure of the concert will be considered and social network publicity arrangements made, will be on Sunday 18th May at Cafe Oto, or Carole's house in Battersea – times and details to be confirmed. At that meeting or before, we'll also decide what other meetings are needed before 28th June to satisfy people's needs.

Please let me know your needs, or any other questions, if you cannot make these meetings. I hope to have a copy of the scores facsimile booklet for everyone on 23rd March, but it may have to be posted out soon after that. The hire of Chisenhale Dance Space is being covered by money made from previous 'Song Books' performances. I am looking forward to this.

Minutes of the inaugural 'Nature Study Notes' Meeting (23 March 2014)

Present: Stefan Szczelkun, Carol Finer, Bron Jones, Robbie Lockwood, Emmanuel Spinelli, Emmanuelle Waeckerle and Portia Winters. Apologies had been received from: Hugh Shrapnel, Jane Alden, Howard Skempton, Carolyn Rogers, Grundik Kasayansky, Martin Dixon, Ali Warner and Sharon Gal.

Lack of trains from South London surprised me, and made me late. So we had a shorter formal meeting than planned, but it was a good one. I handed out photocopies of the original score booklet. After studying the book, we will all come to agreement about how to make a concert using our selections from the rites.

If possible, we will follow up this performance with a future higher profile performance using our own rites in a similar style - so if you think of any new rites, please do write them down. But first we will study and absorb these historic scores, and think about how they can best be realised on June 28th.

We didn't discuss the scores at the meeting, as most people hadn't had time to familiarise themselves with them. What we did do was each talk about what we'd been doing in the last year, and in the process started or continued getting to know each other (two people were new to the group).

The next meeting on Wednesday April 23 at Carole Finer's house is now confirmed, 6-9pm (bring food to share). Also confirmed is the meeting on Sunday May 18th at Cafe Oto, 2-4pm. Two more meetings before the performance on 28th to be arranged at the May meeting - one will be at Chisenhale!

Carol offered her 45-minute Resonance FM radio slot for an illustrated pre-performance discussion on Friday 20th June 3-3.45pm. So, if you want to talk or perform an improvisation rite on live radio, keep this afternoon free. Bron has a performance of her chamber opera 'Room of Worlds' coming up on 9th and 10th May at the Horse Hospital. Please come along! She has written the libretto under her Crass name, Eve Libertine.

We will set up a public Facebook Event for 'Nature Study Notes' to share thoughts and what we are doing. We need a publicity image.

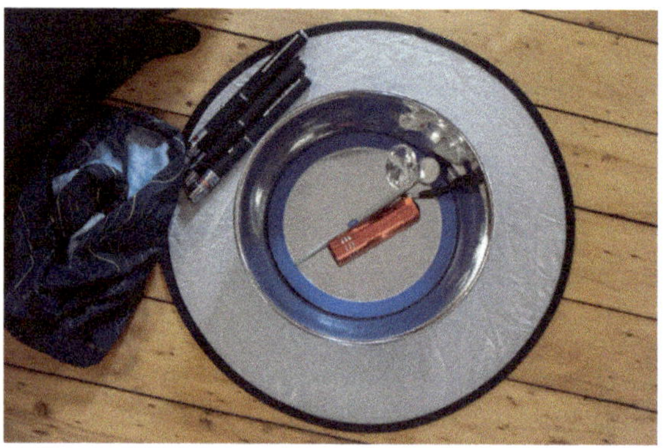

Photography by Martin Dixon

Bron Jones to Stefan (March 2014)

Thanks for this Stefan, and for mentioning the opera! I can't seem to think of much else at the moment - it's a funny business trying to find something from somewhere that feels right, and am letting things slide a bit; like cleaning and gardening and emails... It was lovely to see you again and everyone. I look forward to the next meeting.

Minutes of the Meeting in Battersea (22 April 2014)

Present: Stefan, Emmanuelle, Sharon, Carolyn and Carole.

We talked about the rites for over two hours. Please choose rites that you like, and check the related notes in the back of the booklet. The [following] rites were noted as possible choices by Sharon: 9/18/22/25/26/28/30/34/36/38/50/53/65/68/72 / 80/81/109/113/115/129/137/142.

Questions arising from the discussion: Do most rites require a group rather than individuals to perform them? How do we agree start times? The feeling was that this should happen not by 'orders' or notifications, but maybe by more subtle means. For example, 'landmarks' could be agreed as cues for a group rite to start.

It was agreed that the performance would work better with quite a large number of performers. Stefan pointed out that this was only limited by his time to do administration and arranging for people to meet. There are likely to be from 10 to 20 performers at Chisenhale on the 28th.

Can we perform more than one rite at a time? Yes, but it might be good to have one single rite to start the concert and one to end it. Possibly even use the same one. It has been suggested that to start with Cornelius's Rite 26 would be good (CCSR26): "Everyone sings a song at same time, not necessarily the same song." Or the

Jumping Up and Down rite. Or the Hissing/Snarling rite by David Jackman (DJ68). This would work well theatrically.

A suggestion was made that each participant should choose their favourites before the next meeting. Two weeks before the actual event, we must have made our final decisions. We will draw up a programme with the selected rites, and a final list of performers. Anyone joining after that stage will be expected to follow this plan, at least as far as the planned group rite performances.

Carol pointed out that in the Scratch Orchestra there was a difference between performing a rite as a solo or as an accompaniment. Carol described an accompaniment as 'group sound'.

A visit to the venue would be good. Can this be arranged? Maybe to follow our next meeting.

Rites being performed could be put up on large placards, or projected on a screen. Or these rites could be printed as a programme for the audience. There was some discussion of whether the audience could have any rites to do themselves. Does this idea of transparency, letting the audience understand what score is being used at any moment, take away from the wonder/mystery? This would be different from the Scratch Orchestra days. Transparency wasn't an issue then (as far as I remember).

Can everyone please help with publicity! Many listings require a long lead time i.e. you may have to act now! Hopefully we will be listed in the printed version of *The Wire* – thanks to Sharon! If you know or use a listing service please feed it with the following blurb (edit as needed):

'The Scratch Orchestra's Nature Study Notes' performed by an ensemble of original Scratch Orchestra members and new performers including: Jane Alden, Carole Finer, Sharon Gal, Lucie Galand, John Hails, Bryn Harris, Bron Jones, Robbie Lockwood, Geraldine McEwan, Carolyn Rogers, Hugh Shrapnel, Howard Slater, Emmanuel Spinelli, Stefan Szczelkun, Emmanuelle Waeckerle, Ali Warner and Portia Winters. - 'Nature Study Notes' is a collection of Fluxus-like instructions or 'scores' that was published by Cornelius Cardew at the very beginning of the Scratch Orchestra in 1969. This is a music improvisation and visual performance event of about one hour duration.

Our next meeting is on the 18th May at Cafe Oto from 2-4pm. Please bring your list of preferred rites, or if you can't make the meeting then email them to me with any comments. At this meeting, we'll arrange more meetings prior to the performance on the 28th June.

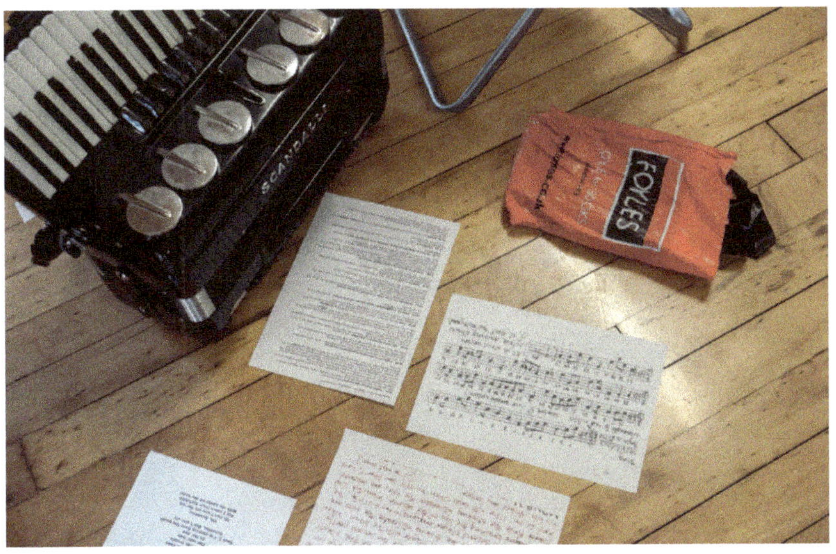

Photograph by Martin Dixon

Stefan to the group (16 May 2014)

Hoping to see many of you for an important 'Nature Study Notes' meeting on Sunday 2-4pm at Cafe Oto.

Agenda: People continuing to get to know each other. Discussing the 'Nature Study Notes' score as applied to the upcoming concert. Preparations for publicity and flyer. Arranging final meetings before concert.

There is now a Facebook Event for the performance:

https://www.facebook.com/events/1422087781384112/

Facebook junkies, please post the rites you like in the Event on Facebook and 'like' others' rite writings. Alright?

Some Posts in the Facebook Event page

Stefan Szczelkun

HMSRIR5 "For any number of people, preferably unknown to each other, making any kind of vocal of physical sound; no instruments to be used. Performance to take place in any large area, inside or outside, with everyone scattered throughout the whole area, widely separated from each other as possible. A person stays in the same place throughout the performance; physical motion of all kind is kept to a minimum. Sounds can be of any kind produced from the person i.e. vocal sounds (singing, speaking, whispering, shouting, crying, laughing hissing, etc.) or from the body (hissing slapping clapping etc.)

Sounds are made in response to other sounds, therefore the

sound made should have some meaning to the person making it. This meaning can be verbal (conversational) or aural (musical), or a combination of both. A response can be immediate (spontaneous reaction to some kind of sound probably verbal) or reflective (probably musical). S/He can also arouse the response of other people by some sounds; or s/he can just listen. In general, the nature of the improvisation should be still and reflective. The performance ends for each person when he has nothing more he wants to do. S/he may then get up and leave, this being the only physical movement he makes." (Hugh Shrapnel)

The notes on p.14 of the 'Nature Study Notes' booklet give this rite a title: 'Improvisation Rite' and give a simpler variant that I quoted earlier: "Replace first 12 lines with: Any number of people making any sounds. Perform in a large area, as widely separated from each other as possible. Performers stay in the same place throughout, keep physical movement to a minimum."

This is an important rite to me and, as I have said, describes a basic form of improvising with a large group. Howard Slater said he used this rite with a group of students in Copenhagen recently.

"Thie stode as thei had bene turned into stones... all was husht and mute... al was as styl as ye midnight... neyther loude nor distincke, but as it were the sounde of a swarme of bees".

Richard III by Thomas More quoted by Hanan Yoran, 2013

The only response possible 'when reality becomes unintelligible'?

Minutes of the meeting at Cafe Oto (18 May 2014)

Present: Geraldine, Emmanuelle, Carol, John, Bron, Robbie, Linn D, Jane, Hugh, Howard and Stefan. Apologies from Ali and Bryn. Sharon works on Sundays.

A good meeting. A lovely group. We started by going around and saying what we'd been doing recently, by way of introductions. Several people were new to each other - Howard Slater, John Hails and Hugh Shrapnel were at a group meeting for the first time. John Hails had come down from Edinburgh.

I summarised our previous discussions at Carol's house, and the rites that were most popular (see list below). Also, the idea we had come to, of us all starting and ending with a single agreed rite. This was discussed and the idea confirmed, apparently unanimously. Later in the meeting, I think we tentatively agreed that we would open with Hugh's Improvisation Rite, as previously circulated, and end with one of two possible singing rites, where we all sing a song of our choice standing in a line facing the audience, i.e. Bryn Harris' rite 35 and/or rite 26 'Before playing all sing a song in unison' (CCSR26). This could possibly be followed by a few minutes of quiet visual activity after each person has finished their song, before the end.

The time between the beginning and ending rites would be for individual or sub-group choices of rites. We discussed several. Only one was agreed. John Hails is to lead a group of six or more of us doing David Jackman's hissing and grotesque-face-pulling at half-time. This is rite 68, and has been quoted above. Other sub-groups can be formed at the remaining meetings, or by individuals agreeing sub-group plans together outside of the group meetings. There could be women's rites, for instance. At the previous meeting, we had discussed the 'Stupid Book' rite (CCSBR7), and Carol had given an example of the prosaic sexism in modernist literature (Emile Zola...). Would you like to lead on this rite, Carol?

I expressed mild concern that the full range of audio dynamics (I was thinking particularly of bass and amplitude) might not be used, with so few of us using amplified electronics or 'instruments' capable of such range. Robbie says he might use electronics? Sharon might use her electric guitar? We could invite an acoustic bass player. Jane will bring her violin. Something to think about.

The role of the audience was discussed. Should they be active or just listening? See Cardew's rite 102: 'Give your instrument to an onlooker... etc' and Hugh Shrapnel's rite 141: "It is all very well to keep silence, but one has also to consider the kind of silence one keeps." (HMSSB141). No definite conclusions where reached on this question.

Rite choices so far:

John Hails: 17, 47, 65, 71, 81, 89, 103, 113, 125, 135

Robbie Lockwood: 1, 9, 11, 21, 22, 29

Emmanuelle: 5, 17, 30, 32, 38, 49, 68, 76, 101, 129, 145, 146

Hugh: 5, 7, 8, 18, 29, 32, 45, 89, 60, 89, 131

Sharon: 9, 18, 22, 25, 26, 28, 30, 34, 36, 38, 50, 53, 65, 68, 72, 80, 81, 109, 113, 115, 129, 137, 142

Carolyn: 5, 7, 18, 26, 25,28, 29, 34, 47, 66, 68, 82, 127, 129, 141, 143, 145

Not a huge amount of agreement comes out of this collection of choices, but if you want to collaborate on any of these with the selectors, please email them personally, not the group. Surprise us! e.g. John and Hugh like rite 89 "Play lying full length on your stomach... etc" by Christopher Hobbs, so they could decide to do this together at some point as a duet. Sharon and Emmanuelle (and others) could do 129 together, or decide to do it at different times. Rite 129 is "Look upward, move backward" by Cornelius Cardew, which possibly suggests a movement of great beauty but could also be interpreted as a metaphor in sound.

If you made verbal points at the meeting that I've not included here, please email me and I'll do a second edition of these minutes.

I had a visual idea that there could be complimentary tickets for friends who would agree to sit on cushions in the performance area, covered with a veil or net curtain. I was surprised that the idea was well received. I'm planning to do a version of Cardew's rite 25 'Reflect' using pen lasers, an LED torch and a mirrored tin bowl with some water in it.

I forgot to discuss publicity. I'm hoping Ali Warner will do a drawing, which we'd include on a paper flyer. [Her drawing is in the introduction above.] Anyone can contribute flyers or words, especially in the Event on Facebook, but also via email.

It is about two or three weeks before the performance, I hope you will all personally email your entire address book to invite them. That is our collective power and in any case the only choice, as there is no publicity budget.

Another thing I forgot is to ask is if anyone knows newspaper reviewers or radio producers to invite personally. To go further with this project, we need this kind of attention from critics.

Forthcoming meetings and Carol's radio show for your diaries:

Sunday 15th June at Bron's place, 7-9pm, London N16

Friday 20th June, c. 2-2.45pm, Carol's Resonance FM radio show. Please contact Carol if you'd like to help on that e.g. reading or performing rites.

Saturday 21st June meeting at Carol's house in Battersea, 6.30-9pm.

Performance on 28th June. Get there at 6.30pm prompt! There will be a warm-up at 7pm, doors open at 7.30pm. Please visit Chisenhale before the performance, if you can.

Hugh Shrapnel to the group (20 May 2014)

Hi Stefan and everyone. Yes, good meeting and good minutes. Just some little additions. I think we thought it would be good to do the 'Immaculate Conception' rite by Michael Chant (MCICR60): 'Throughout the rite sway from side to side'. Also, Robbie suggested (my) commentary rite: 'One person from the gathering is elected as a speaker to commentate on anything (something, many things) present' for right at the end after the singing, to comment on what's going on (HMSCR104).

Re: the publicity, it's a small point, but I think it's possibly a bit misleading to link the rites with Fluxus, as the rites are about collective/group activity (which is what the Scratch Orchestra was about), whereas Fluxus was about something else i.e. Fluxus!

———

More posts in the Facebook Event Page

Stefan Szczelkun (20 May 2014)

I came across this quote, and I'm not sure how true this is in relation to orchestral music: "What is the difference between the star-system and the ensemble approach to theatre? In the star system, the production is built around the lead actor, the 'star'. [Often], he would have owned the company. His wife was usually the leading lady, and his son and daughter would often play the 'romantic' leads. Plays were selected to show off the star's talents. The supporting cast was there to assist the star. Typically, the audience came to see the star. In the ensemble approach, there are no stars. There are leading roles, simply because that's the way plays are written. But the actor who played the lead in one production, would have a supporting role in the next show. In the star system, the star played all of the leads, all the time. In an ensemble production, the audience came to see the play, not the star. The person responsible for moulding a company of actors into an ensemble is the director."

Two men brought about the shift from the star-system to the ensemble approach in theatre: Richard Wagner (1813-1883) and Georg, the Duke of Saxe-Meiningen (1826-1914).

http://www3.northern.edu/wild/th100/_Chapt8a.htm

Stefan Szczelkun (30 May 2014)

Quote from current reading, recommended to me by Anthony Iles: "Everything in the aesthetic State, even the subservient tool, is a free citizen having equal rights with the noblest; and the intellect, which forcibly moulds the passive multitude to its designs, must here ask for its assent." (Friedrich Schiller re the French Revolution in 1795)

George Chambers (18 June 2014)

On Saturday, I will be performing HMSIR43, which entails walking from Greenwich Pier to the Woolwich dockyard, picking up stray items I find on the way. The walk is about 5 miles and I'm going to take photos en route, which will form a slideshow for our performance on 28th. If anyone would like to join me on the walk, it would be lovely to see some of you there. I'll be at Greenwich pier at 12.00. The walk is about 5.5 miles. If that's too much, halfway there is North Greenwich station where you could depart the walk. I'll probably stop off at one or two strategic watering holes on the way. Do message me if you fancy it!

Stefan Szczelkun (23 June 2014)

A slip of paper with the following undated quote by Howard Slater slipped out of Eddie Prevost's first book: "Our improvising, it seems to me, is a matter of entering into relation in the widest possible way: relation with our unconscious, a relation with our materials and expression, a relation with the medium of expression, a relation with imagination, a relation with the recipient of our attempted communications etc. The wider the scope of potential relation then the more possibilities there are to both come across ways in which our activity and expression is determined (by the hidden social messages in language, by the technique of virtuosity, by the closure of product) and to modify and change this determination; to maintain that the social is never fully determined, and its potential for freedom is never closed but persists as the outcome of experimentalism."

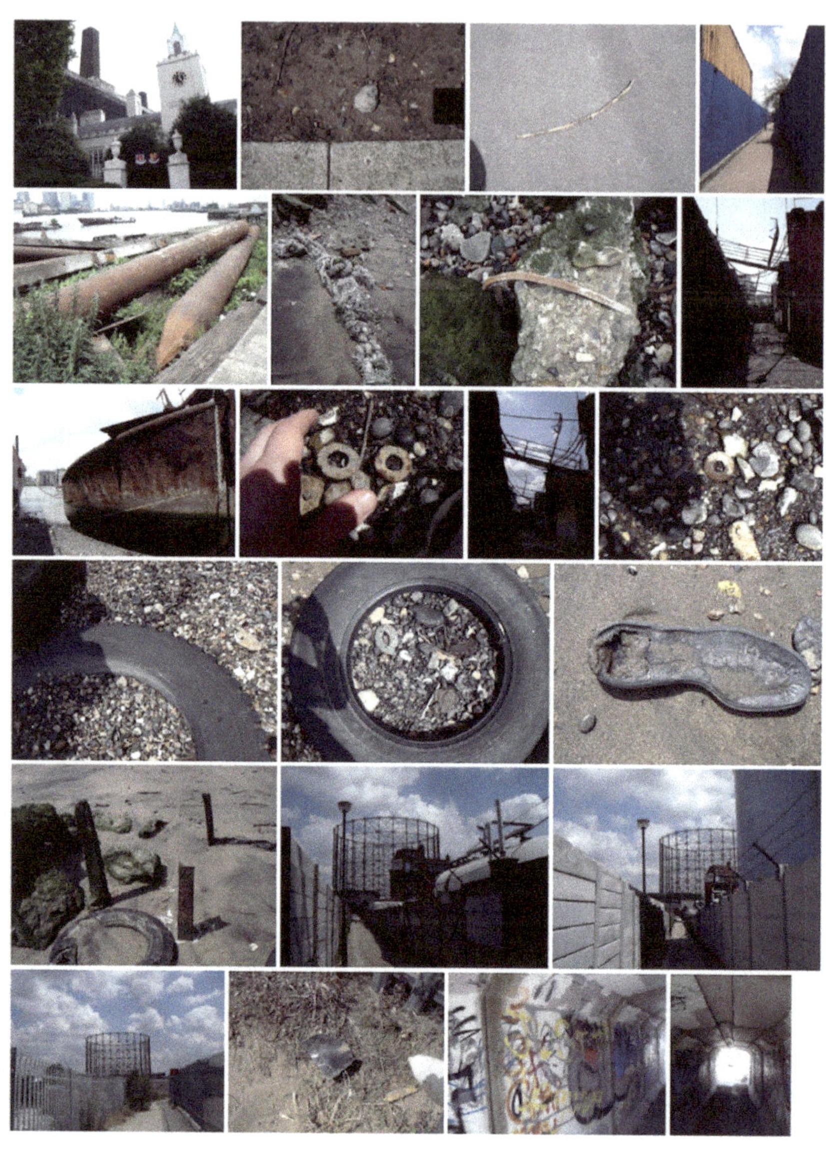

Photos by George Chambers

Note: George Chambers performed the rite with composer Hugh Shrapnel on Saturday 21 June.

Chapter 2 Section 1

Nature Study Notes 1: Chisenhale Dance Space

PRESS RELEASE

The Scratch Orchestra's Nature Study Notes at Chisenhale Dance Space

Saturday 28th June 2014 7.30pm 64-84 Chisenhale Rd, London E3 £5.50

'The Scratch Orchestra's Nature Study Notes' – performed by an ensemble of original Scratch Orchestra members and new performers including: Jane Alden, George Chambers, Carole Finer, Sharon Gal, John Hails, Bryn Harris, Eve Libertine, Robbie Lockwood, Geraldine McEwan, Linn D, Hugh Shrapnel, Howard Slater, Stefan Szczelkun, Emmanuelle Waeckerle, Ali Warner.

Nature Study Notes is a collection of 152 written instructions or 'scores' that was published by Cornelius Cardew at the very beginning of the Scratch Orchestra in 1969. This is a music improvisation and visual performance event about one hour duration.

It is unlikely that tickets will be available on the night as seating is limited. Phone Chisenhale to check. To be sure of admission please book.

Rites on the night will include Cornelius Cardew's 'Stupid Book Rite' and his 'The Sheet of Water' rite, Tim Mitchell's 'Tube Train Rite' ('Mark out a journey...'), also Frederic Rzewski's 'Les Moutons de Panurge' for musicians & non-musicians (Suggested Theme for non-musicians: "The left hand doesn't know what the right hand is doing") and Carole Finer's 'Improvisation Rite No. 2 Flower Music' - and many others. (Ali Warner 3-6-14)

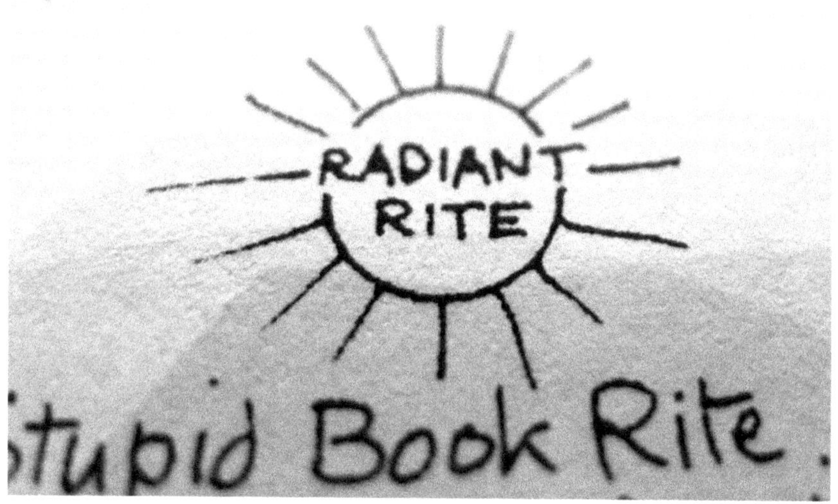

Photo by Emmanuelle Waeckerle

The Resonance Radio Show (20 June 2014)

Hear ye! Hear Ye! The Nature Study Notes Radio Show

It is on this Friday at 3 until 3.45pm on Resonance Radio, 104.4 Fm or online, with host Carole Chant Finer and guests Hugh Shrapnel and Jane Alden, who will be discussing 'Nature Study Notes' in the context of text based scores, Fluxus and the revolutionary atmosphere of the late Sixties. They will be joined by Charles Celeste Hutchins, Stefan Szczelkun, Geraldine McEwan, Ali Warner and maybe others for a live on-air performance of 'Mountain Rite' CCCMR75. "Find, or make a mountain. From the top blow your problems and solutions to the (four) winds".

https://soundcloud.com/nethersage/sound-out-140620-nss

Nature Study Notes Meeting at Carole Finer's house (21 June 2014)

Present: Carole, Jane, May, Les, George, Robbie and Stefan.

There had also been the meeting before the radio show the day before and even the show itself was part of our exchanges. Thanks to Carole for her professional hosting. It was a very varied bunch of people and Carole graciously including everyone in the 45mins of globally broadcast live transmission. The programme will be repeated at 8am this Monday.

An interesting point that came out from Bryn and Hugh was that the rites were originally intended as a way to prepare the group mind preceding improvisation; rather than being compositions in themselves. As it turned out many of the contributions are more like compositions. So 'Nature Study Notes' as a collection contains this tension.

After some wider discussion, eating and looking at Ali's spreadsheet of people's choices the meeting came to the conclusion that some programming was necessary to avoid possible clashes between the most popular rites. We made a list of the most popular rites, that we defined as those with 4 or more people signed up to them. Each of the most popular rites was then discussed and assigned a start time in the performance.

I put this up on our Facebook page as we are unlikely to have a programme on the night. This would give those who want to know more details of what we were doing. And it can be amended after the performance.

https://www.facebook.com/events/1422087781384112/

The rough programme was made so that popular rites that people wanted to do at the same time or which specified a group performance, didn't clash. Other rites to be played by individuals, duos or trios are not listed below. This programming is a new departure from the procedures of the original Scratch Orchestra Concerts in which a programme was usually designed by one person - starting with the youngest member.

Skeletal Programme

20.00 HMSIR 5 led by Hugh Shrapnel starts the concert. When this ends we do rite CCAR17 'accompaniment and solo'.

20.09 ABP 128 Co-ordinated by Jane Alden. '9 basic sounds'

20.16 CCSR 18 'Elected soloist repeats an action' Ali Warner leads

20.25 HSBR 34 'Six deep breaths' (group version) led by Bryn Harris. NB dispersed in time version led by Sharon Gal.

20.27 CFIRNTFM 145 'Flower piece' co-ordinated by Carolyn.

20.29 DJ 68 led by John Hails 'Slow metamorphosis to a snarling mob'

20.36 CCRR 66 Co-ordinated by Carolyn 'Radiant rite'

20.40 FRLMDP 47 Conducted by George Chambers 'musical notation'

20.48 CCAMMR 129 ‘Look upward, move backward’, ensemble version co-ordinated by Sharon Gal

20.54 BHUSR 35 ‘Sing our own song finale facing the audience in a line’ led by Stefan who will signal the start.

c20.57 After completing your song return to the space and continue quiet or visual improvising.

21.00 Quiet ending.

21.30 Take our leave.

These are guide times only and are not meant to be measured to the second. Any other rites as solo, duets or trios may be done anytime you like. CCSBR 7 ‘Stupid book rite’ may have more than 3 performers but Carol didn’t want a group start time - respond to her. Don’t forget to enjoy some silences. And, of course, listen!

There won't be a printed programme as such at the venue so this gives some idea/record of what occurred for those that came, and those that didn’t.

Links to a Recording and Photographs of the performance at Chisenhale

https://flic.kr/s/aHsjZgASke

Our photographer was Martin Dixon. His photographs are used in this chapter and the previous one.

https://soundcloud.com/nethersage/nss-140628-simple-stereo-mixdown

Sound recorded by Bryn Harris. Play it whilst reading reviews?

Review of 'Nature Study Notes' Ben Harper (3 July 2014)

Boring Like A Drill Blog

Non-systems (1)

On Saturday, I got to see and hear the Scratch Orchestra play selections from Nature Study Notes. I saw these guys performing Cage's Song Books a couple of years ago, and again there was a blurring between art and life. Performers would come and go, participate when they felt most at home with the material, occasionally opting out to sit in the stalls with the audience or stand on the stairs outside. The door to the fire escape stayed open, letting in sounds from the surrounding streets and houses.

Much of the material in the Notes is open to interpretation and speculation. Reading over them after the event, it's fun to spot how many you can recognise.

I learned later that there had been some general discussion of ideas beforehand, but no group rehearsal. The nature of the Scratch Orchestra music, as alluded to in the notes themselves, had little of the focused intensity of activity found in Cage's music. An atmosphere of informality and naturalism was sustained throughout – this was achieved largely through the sensitivity and dedication of the performers to the spirit in which the Notes were made. As when observing a street scene, everything that happened in front of the audience fell together into its own sense of order.

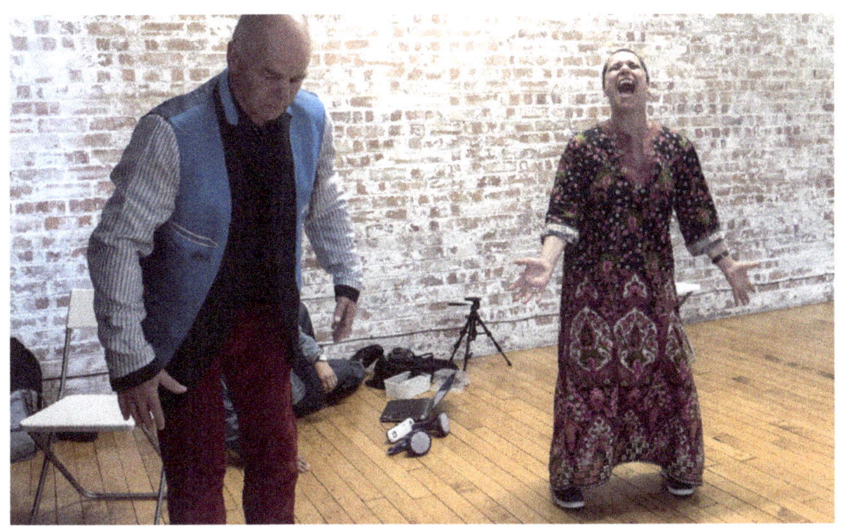

Photograph - Martin Dixon

Review of 'Nature Study Notes' Phil England (November 2014)

The Wire #369

"The fluid relationships and community-forming engendered by tonight's performance can be seen as a rehearsal for the peaceful coexistence and non-judgemental acceptance needed to supersede the competitive anxiety that characterizes current financialised interrelations."

The whole review can be seen here:

http://martindx.blogspot.co.uk/2014/10/one-of-three-scratch-orchestra-review.html?spref=fb

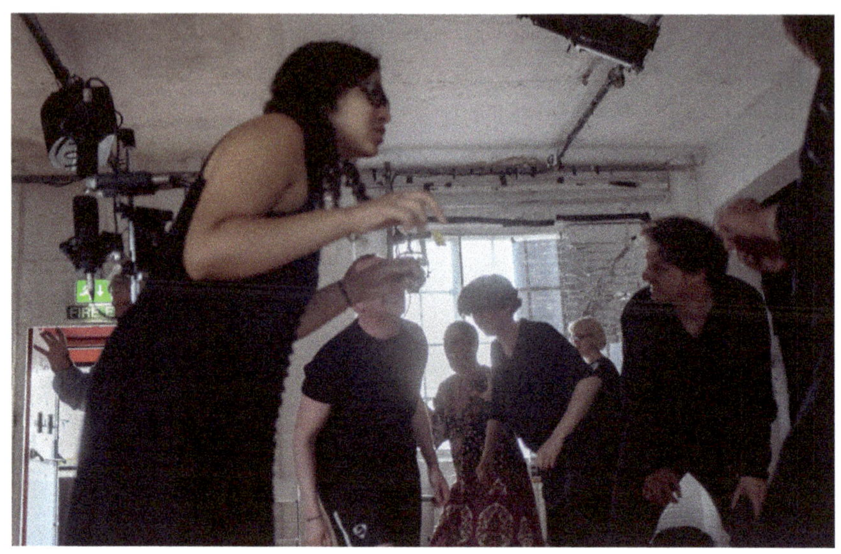

Photograph - Martin Dixon

Review of 'Nature Study Notes' Penny Homer (30 June 2014)

'Up To Scratch' - Bachtrack

Formed in 1969 by Cornelius Cardew, along with Howard Skempton and Michael Parsons, the Scratch Orchestra was a reflection of Cardew's experimental philosophy at the time. Anyone could join, as graphic scores were used rather than traditional notation, and improvisation was a major part of any performance. Forty-five years later, the philosophy continues; original Scratch Orchestra members joined with new performers for a new interpretation of Nature Study Notes on Saturday June 28th.

Nature Study Notes is a collection of 152 written instructions or rites for improvisation. How these are presented depends on the performers involved in a specific performance.

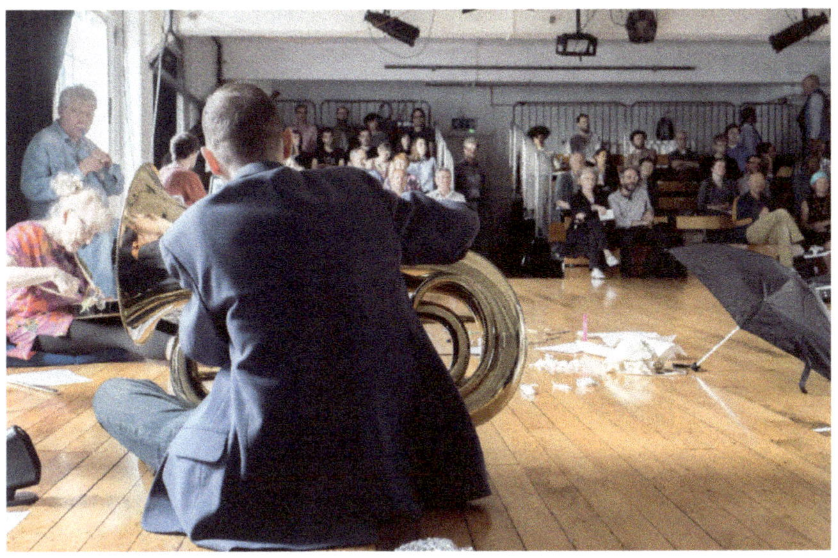

Photograph - Martin Dixon

Chisenhale Dance Space provided a relaxed, informal setting, and the group were similarly relaxed, in a variety of outfits with a variety of props. And so, the scene was set for an hour of hugely inventive and highly imaginative performance from an extremely talented group.

What really came across as the hour unfolded was the sense of travel. There was ebb and flow, with several climactic moments building towards a final zenith near the end of an hour. It was also an auditory and visual feast – to give an idea, here are just a few examples of the sounds and sights I experienced; a music box, someone dressing in bubble wrap, throat clearing, scrawling with a marker pen, face washing, breathing through a tuba and reading from Zola.

The performance made the most of the space as well, moving

about it to bring contrast and meaning to the visual and sonic effects. At times it was curiously relaxing, and if I hadn't been enjoying what I was seeing so much, I would have closed my eyes to let the sounds wash over me. In other places my senses were heightened, and I became very aware of the details of each performer's rite.

It also felt very true to the title; even when there was digital and technical manipulation the performance felt very naturalistic. There were night-time scenes, tribal climaxes and jungle sounds. The only swerve away from this was about halfway through, where a repeated gesture and sound (digitally manipulated to produce varied echoes) stage front brought us a little too close to pastiche. Otherwise, it all felt incredibly fresh, thanks to complete commitment of the entire group. Everyone looked like they were having a lot of fun, and I felt a very strong temptation to get up and start walking around, so much did Cardew's ethos seem to be in practice.

As things drew to a close, the open fire-escape brought a wonderful addition as birdsong filled the space, which was darkening under the dusk. The performance faded into the nothingness from which it had emerged, and we sat in hushed silence for some minutes, enjoying the stillness. It is impossible to capture the details of such an experience in words, and of course another performance would be an entirely different experience. But this is the beauty of it; I hope very much that this is not a one-off performance and that there will be opportunities to see Nature Study Notes again in the near future.

https://bachtrack.com/review-scratch-nature-study-notes-june-2014

Post-Chisenhale Performance

Stefan Szczelkun to Group (July 2014)

Could we meet this Sunday at Emmanuelle's new house in Thornton Heath? Say 3 – 6pm. Bring a bottle (not necessarily alcohol).

The financial position was OK. Income from having 37 paying audience members was £185 (from We Got Tickets) and space hire was £150 plus a £100 deposit that was returned. The booklets cost £1 each, so we made a small loss but that is covered by the money we made at Oto and I have plenty of booklets to take forward. So that is all OK – we are in the black.

The news is that Oto have given us a date in February 2015 – Sunday the 22nd. I could have gone for the Friday or Saturday but plumped for Sunday again. This time we are not hiring the space and instead take a 50/50 split of the door. They want publicity details by September so if you can give a definite commitment to that date please let me know. If its an 'almost definite' let me know as well!

So we'll have a series of meetings in the autumn to prepare for that probably roughly one a month from October. Let me know the dates you are in London and we'll try to accommodate those who don't live here etc.

I was impressed by everyone's contributions at the performance. Seemed like most of the time we were all listening and having good judgement on when and how to act. Thank you!

I think I was relieved that the rites still work well to direct a collective artwork. Hugh Shrapnel exclaimed after the performance: "I do love Scratch Music!" It meant a lot to me because it meant that we'd captured the spirit of the thing successfully.

Geraldine to Stefan (5 July 2014)

Good morning Stefan,

I am unable to attend the meeting tomorrow. I hope all goes well.

To add my notes -

- As always, the group dynamic worked sensitively with controlled energy

- I was happy with the rites I had chosen. I gave myself enough time to be able to calmly portray my rites while still observing others work.

- I enjoyed going into the audience on two occasions to break the barrier between them and the "performance".

- Audience were happy to leave with something (photos found on chairs and Bob Dylan lyrics I handed out)

- The variety of styles brought by the group was as far reaching as previous performances.

- I love working with this group - it challenges me in ways i'm rather uncomfortable with and I appreciate the relaxed and inclusive attitude of the group.

- I thought there were some magical moments throughout. I have already described one with the lights as a group played notated rites.

- Friends who attended the concert thought it was good throughout and will be attending the second performance in Cafe Oto, as they liked it that much!

Geraldine to group (17 July 2014)

Subject: New space proposed

May I suggest a space for performance / workshop / meetings. The owner is a fabulous friend of mine. I think it's a nicer space than Oto with great mailing list.

Please consider The Apiary Studios. I will be meeting the owner for event planning. I would love to suggest the Scratch Orchestra for a Autumn event. I would think I'd be able to arrange a no-fee hire.

I will get back to you with dates.

Stefan to group (July 2014)

Subject: To be Scratch or to play Scratch

Geraldine's email prompts me to write sooner than I'd intended. I need to make some points.

1. This group, or sub-groups of it, should not really be called 'The Scratch Orchestra'. That could get up a lot of people's noses I reckon. We have been performing The Scratch Orchestra's 'Nature Study Notes', with performers that include original members but that doesn't mean we are 'The' Scratch Orchestra. We were called that in a review, and it's easy to see how it happens, but I don't think we can formally embrace it. The group has had discussions about having a name but couldn't think of one.

2. I had intended to call monthly meetings from early October in Oto on Sunday and another place like Carol's house on a weekday evening; or even on specific dates to suite people who only occasionally come to London, like John Hails. These venues were chosen because they are well-known and with good transport links for all London.

3. I would prefer other venues and performances to be discussed and decided at one of these meetings and by email. If we don't do this, the project we been evolving will, from my point of view, lose its coherence. That in itself can be discussed. This is not to suggest that if Geraldine or anyone else organises an event performing Scratch Music or improvisation rites that it can't happen as an independent project.

4. Oto is not a perfect performance space for us but it is the leading London venue for experimental music that relates to AMM/ Scratch type stuff. Its importance is to do with its cultural status rather than the space itself. Working outside of venues with some kind of widely known identity can easily dissipate the impact of our work.

Chapter 2 Section 2

Nature Study Notes 2 - Cafe Oto 2015

Scratch Orchestra improvisation at Cafe Oto

Stefan to Martin Dixon (8 August 2014)

I was wondering if you would particularly want like to take photos again at our Nature Study Notes performance at Cafe Oto on the evening of the 22nd February?

I had an idea of taking face portraits of all the performers whilst they were performing. Light is a problem unless there was a 'lighting booth' in the corner as part of the performance.

The space is going to be quite dark and lit only with 5 or 6 spotlights shining vertically up at the ceiling. Might be able to make postcards of each portrait as a way of me thanking the performers.

Obviously, you did a great job for us before and I'm very glad of that record. So, maybe it's a bit much asking you again!!

Then again it might almost be unfriendly if I didn't ask!!

Stefan email to group (September 2014)

Hi, all you Nature Study Notes performers, I hope you had a good summer and are enjoying the balmy autumn. Here is a list of three group meetings coming up on Sunday afternoons at Cafe Oto.

12th October 2 - 4pm 2014

16th November 2pm

7th December 2pm

I hope you can make at least one of these meetings. Even if you can't you are still welcome to take part and I will arrange two or three meetings in January and February 2015 in the run up to the Cafe Oto performance, which is on the evening of the 22nd of February. These meeting will be arranged to be as inclusive of everyone as we can be so please keep in touch.

I'm giving all your names as performers to Oto in the next day or so, so please hit reply now if you don't want to be listed on some distant Cafe Oto webpage!

The performance of 'Nature Study Notes' at Chisenhale was immensely satisfying and I see no reason why this quality, coherence and freshness of improvising should not be repeated in February at Oto. I look forward to the people who could not be part of that performance being a part of the new one and contributing their own moments of beauty and drama.

In the first or second meeting Robbie will lead a discussion of the politics inherent to our group and probably there will be echoes and memories of the politics of the Scratch Orchestra.

Looking forward to see you all very much indeed!

Please RSVP even if just say yay or nay.

Minutes of meeting (12 October 2014)

Present: Geraldine, Robbie, Bron, Carole and Stefan.

We first caught up with what each of us had been up to - briefly!

Eddie Prevost's improvisation workshop was where several people met first. It was still happening on Friday evenings in The Welsh Chapel Hall hear Borough, for a contribution of £5. It could be a place where people who want to 'practice' improvising together could go.

Bron said she had had difficulty getting into reading the Rites; they were so small and tightly packed. The next meeting on 7th December will be at Bron's place and will be a practical workshop on rite playing!

Robbie would like to discuss the change in political landscape and context between when the rites were first written and used, and now. Robbie and Carole are going to contact Ali (who can't come on Sundays...) We will also invite Chris Hobbs and Virginia Anderson to this meeting.

Ali offered to lead a discussion of 'how to structure the development/group process' ... but cannot make it on Sundays.

Stefan to Hugh Shrapnel (6 November 2014)

Subject: Re: Nature Study Notes improvisation at Cafe Oto on 22nd February 2015

Hi Hugh, Good to hear from you. Look forward to meeting on December the 7th, hopefully!

I'm glad you want to take part again and I'd value your input into the development process. I'm thinking maybe we should introduce a theme of some kind. As in Scratch concerts. Also, to make it so it doesn't repeat the same approach to 'Nature Study Notes' again. My first thought was 'Rites of Spring' (re-done as a 'popular' classic) as having obvious relationships to 'Nature Study Notes'. What do you think about this? I'd appreciate any ideas you have to bring to this next meeting.

What did you think of the review in The Wire?

Hugh to Stefan (7 November 2014)

Thanks for your message.

I saw Carolyn yesterday and we had a chat about the Nature Study notes performance.

We weren't sure about having a theme as it could either impose too much (which wouldn't be good) or not at all (in which case it would serve no purpose). Carolyn thought that rather than having a theme as such, it is much more important to think about presentation – carefully considering the particularities of the Cafe Oto in that its a very different venue from Chisenhale, it has a concrete floor (unlike the wooden one at Chisenhale), there is not much floor space but lots of chairs and tables and its quite dark. We would therefore have a different relation to the audience. Because of the limited floor space Carolyn suggested using the tables, while I thought using torches (because of the darkness) might be good.

Overall, we thought that because the venue is so different we felt that the performance would also be very different even if we did the same rites again. We favoured having a similar approach to Chisenhale, i.e. people coming together for certain rites as well as separating. Carolyn said she wanted to do the rites she did at Chisenhale again.

Hope this is useful!

Carolyn can't get to the meetings but will continue to think about presentation but I hope to come on the 7th. Do pass it onto the others if you like unless you think it best to hold on till the 7th.

Minutes of Meeting (16 November 2014)

Present: Bron, Carole, Matt, Les, Emmanuelle, Stefan. Apologies from Robbie, Hugh, Carolyn, Geraldine, and probably others!

Discussed Hugh's email to Stefan (including discussion with Carolyn) and Hugh's suggestion of torches. It was decided, unless overturned by a stronger idea later, to light the Oto space with upward facing large LED spotlight type torches mounted in cardboard (or other) tubes to avoid glare. These would light the low, white Oto ceiling and generate enough indirect light to work by. Lights would be turned on only when playing or to another pattern. Along with the existing white columns in the space and any personal lighting that people need, these up-lights should create a dramatically lit and dynamic environment. Stefan will buy a set of these spotlights beforehand and will bring a sample spotlight to the next meeting.

Discussed: My proposal to write new rites. I read out three that I have written and I asked what associations arose in people minds. Newly written rites will be a supplement to the 152 original rites and compositions. Please send them to me (no more than six please!) and I will compile them. New rites will only be used in the performance if they are freely chosen. i.e. people may choose to stick with the original list.

Stefan's new rites:

* Fire comes from heaven. As preparation, an image may be drawn or downloaded.

* Before coming in, please wipe your feet. (metaphoric use preferred,

but can be performed as an instruction)

* Choose a jingling combination like 'willy nilly' and make up a sentence to declaim to the audience in the manner of a street-corner orator or busker.

You do not have to use any of these of course. But please do refer to the facsimile 'Nature Study Notes' booklet.

It was generally agreed, for the time being, NOT to have a theme (or evocative title) for the performance.

Hopefully Ali will be able to set up a similar method for choices of rites to be co-ordinated as before (An online spreadsheet). So that clusters of performers who choose the same rite may choose to play that rite at a particular programmed start time. This worked very well before.

We discussed the nature of the everyday improvisation that precedes the creation of new meanings underpinning the dynamism of ordinary language. Everyone is open to this all of the time - if they are willing to let go of rigidified ideas and neo-classical norms.

Improvisation often goes through boring periods before something exciting happens (Les). But with a larger group maybe the boring bits can be quiet and the good bits distributed in time so a performance has a better overall quality?

We booked a pre-performance live radio show with Carol Finer on Resonance Radio for Friday the 20th February at 2pm. Please put this date in your diary.

Chris Hobbs and Virginia Anderson are intending to take part in the performance and hopefully will attend a meeting or two early in the New Year.

Rough Accounts - Notes

The last two performances basically just covered their costs. The first performance of Cage's 'Song Books' at Oto made money and some people claimed a share but Stefan kept the rest to enable future performances to cover losses and pay deposits etc.

I haven't kept very good accounts - sorry - but this leaves about £650 for the group to use to promote future activity. I will buy some high-power spotlights from this fund at Carol's suggestion.

I suggest the income from the upcoming Oto performance be distributed equally amongst the performers soon after I get it, unless there is another suggestion. e.g. publishing a CD. However, this would need a x4 channel recording at least with proper mix down edit. The recording of the Chisenhale performance from one mike probably does not capture enough of what was a very spread out performance.

Financial arrangement with Oto

We will each get a complimentary ticket up to a max of 20. The ticket price set by Oto will be £7 in advance, with £9 on the door (£6 to Oto members). We get 70% of ticket sales income.

Oto will do their usual publicity although it would be useful to have a F*bk event page sometime soon; as we can use it to share ideas and messages as well. (I don't have a record of how many of the participants use F*Bk or of those who don't.)

Next Meeting is at Bron's place in London N16. We will be playing and no doubt talking about our initial choices. Bron has chosen the fingernail painting rite and Stefan wants to do Carol's rite number 146 using the Newspaper of the day. Hopefully some more new rites will arrive that we can try.

Bron Jones to Stefan (24 November 2014)

Just found this in drafts. I thought I'd sent it last week! Thanks for excellent minutes Stefan. You're a very good leader of the group, even if we don't have a leader! You seem to have a calm and complete trust that it will all happen each time and that seems to allow everyone to find their place. It's a rare gift. See you at mine on 7th.

Nature Study Notes Meeting (7 December 2014)

Present: Les, Bron, Carol, Matt, Petri, Emmanuelle, Stefan.
Apologies received from: Chris Hobbs and Virginia Anderson, George, Hugh, Geraldine, Ali, Jane, Carolyn and Robbie. Also, Bryn.

This was a satisfying meeting. Thanks for Bron for the venue and the mulled wine and teas.

People arrived slowly so we had some time getting to know the new person, Petri, who comes via Emmanuelle. He is a guitar player and improviser. Welcome to the group Petri!

We talked about the freedom of improvised music. The rites weren't a set of rules. Matt put a view that there are many other implicitly agreed or decided things that put complete 'freedom' at arms-length.

When most people had arrived, we did a 'check-in', which is when everyone can speak in turn about anything they need to 'get off their chest', without interruption or anyone else commenting. Everyone seemed to self-discipline in how much time they took, and that seemed to produce an emotional closeness between the group and also cleared our minds somewhat to talk about what we came together for – music making.

Then I asked for people thoughts on the 'Nature Study Notes' rites and whether people had any ideas for new rites. Again, people spoke in turn although now of course people could interpose comments and follow up ideas. This is the summary. More precise details of the new rites will follow early in the new year.

Les: He introduced some new rites he had composed:

- *Set Strategy Rite*: Pair up with another person. They do not need to be doing this rite also. Listen to their playing and pick out three parameters. (For example: pitch, speed, duration, timbre, etc.) For each of your three parameters, try to either match your partner or do the complete opposite of them.

- *Pop Rite*: Pick any pop song which is relatively current and which contains instructions to the user on how to act, dance, sing, clap, etc, and follow these instructions outside of the song's context.

- *Green Rite*: Reduce, re-use, recycle."

Les is also making a one minute sound composition of rite CCR76 for me to use in the performance (I will pay him £8 in line with his project to make one minute compositions for whoever orders one)

Bron: Rites from the blue NSN book that she liked were: 2 - 'fingernails rite', 19 - 'lip brushing rite', 24 - silver pyramid, 26 - 'unison' and rite 30, which we later all played.

Carol: She talked about doing the Stupid Book rite again. She brandished a garish paperback of Emile Zola's 'Therese Raquin'. She might use a megaphone this time. A cardboard one was suggested. Who wants to grab the book from her (as suggested in the rite notes)? Carol had a new rite: 'Count to 10; slowly'.

Matt: He liked rite 91 by Christopher Hobbs and told an enchanting story of seeing a pointed leaf fall onto a moving record. The point had engaged the grooves and the melody was being quietly amplified by the leaf. Les suggested that a cactus thorn and a polystyrene cup could produce a similar effect. Matt also liked rite 36 by Bryn Harris - 'Imagine a score and play it'. Later we played this one together.

Petri: He liked a rite where you played the wrong notes – rite number 123 by Alan Brett. Is a certain sort of virtuosity required?

Emmanuelle: She liked the Silver pyramid rite by Cardew (24) and the lips one, The Small Brush rite by Christopher Hobbs (19), also liked by Bron. Emmanuelle also favoured rites 41, 122, 135 and Carol's 146, which was to use the newspaper of the day. She had also written three new rites:

- Choose a lullaby.
- Jam teeth and mouth open with finger and thumb and then try to say: "I love you" and "Kiss me".
- Pretend to speak fluent Arabic (Emmanuelle spoke fluent Arabic in her childhood).

Some us thought that this could be problematic as it could be taken as an insult, if performed by a non-Arabic speaker. There was a discussion... Carol said she'd read from a phrase book that she had. We agreed that this was a good way of doing this.

Stefan: I was planning to do The Newspaper rite (146). I intended to make a large cone out of the Sunday Time (Les offered to supply copies he can get free) and to stand inside it. Very large sharp paper scissors, attached to a contact mike, would then be used to cut myself free and maybe to cut out sections to read out. It was joked that I was attention seeking. Maybe! I prefer to think I'm keen to have the chance to oppose the hegemony of the newspapers. I had talked earlier about finding a large abandoned umbrella and I had taken the fabric off for an artwork. The skeleton made some nice jangling and was visually arresting in its movement. Les suggested this idea fitted his 'recycle' rite. Bron imagined noise making objects jingling from it. I had one new rite: 'At last! A chance to sew on that loose button. Make sure you can see what you are doing!'

All our new rites can be published on our public Facebook event page. Please send me carefully composed wording or put them up yourself.

I suggested people could make posters. Perhaps with an image from what they were using and the text of a rite they are doing, but, anything you want to say goes. I propose putting the posters up on Cafe Oto walls on the night.

We were then served very tasty mulled wine home-made by Bron. We decided to play one of the rites together (30) and it was good to be playing music together. We tried another and it was even better (36). We should probably record ourselves playing some individual rites for use in Carole's radio show.

As we left Penny Rimbaud came down from upstairs and it was nice to greet him before we left.

So good to have all these elements in the meeting: check-in, consideration of rites and new rites, music making. I had a sense of a solid meeting and it gave me a lot of confidence that people were thinking well about the work.

Dates of meetings for 2015

- Sunday the 25th January at Oto, 2 - 4pm. Try out some lights in the space? Wednesday in the evening of the 4th February at Carole's House, near Clapham Junction (with Ali), and Sunday the 15th February at Cafe Oto 2 - 4pm.

If you cannot make any of these dates please contact me and an extra date will be made that you can get to.

There will be a pre-performance live radio show with Carol Finer on Resonance Radio on Friday the 20th February at 2pm. Meeting beforehand to talk at 1pm in the nearby coffee shop?

The performance at Cafe Oto is the evening of Sunday 22nd February. Just remember:

"No sound is innocent" (Title of a book by Eddie Prevost.)

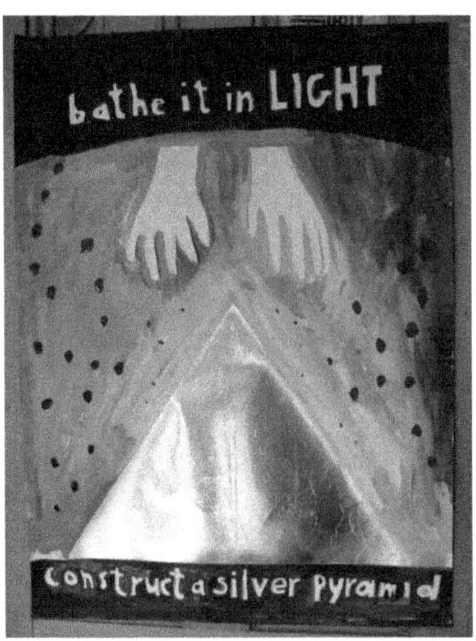

Poster by Bron Jones

Geraldine, could you please set up a Facebook event page again? Ali, could you put up the spreadsheet for us to be able to compare people's choices of rites? Will people be able to add their own new rites to the spreadsheet?

Ali Warner to Group (9 January 2015)

Nice to hear about our last meeting - thanks so much for the notes.

Hope you all had a good/restful/celebratory festive season and are gently entering the New Year.

Rite Selections Tracking Tool. You can find our Rite Selections tracker by following the link provided. (see illustrations below.) This is the same document that I shared before, so lots of you will already have access to it. Please let me know if you have any difficulties getting into this shared document.

Please enter your initials along the row for each of your selected Rites! Each player has a column to themselves.

There are now two pages; the first one, that shows up when you go into the doc, is for our next event in February (marked February 2015). If you want to be reminded what we/you did or which Rites you selected for the performance last June, then click on the grey box at the bottom left that says June 2014 and it will switch pages so you can see last year's completed tracker. Click on the now grey box saying February 2015 to switch back. (These boxes are not shown on the illustrations below.)

I've left a few main rites in pink as before so we can remember which ones are the group ones we performed last June (assuming we might want to do something different this time) – but anyone can feel free to re-colour the pink or have a blank sheet if you prefer!

We can create our own Rites on here – simply scroll down to the last Rite (currently Rite 152) and type in the next consecutive number, the name of your Rite, your name etc. A link in blue goes to another page in which the text of the new rites can be entered in full.

I think we should start creating our own new Rites! I hope that helps, and look forward to seeing you on 4th February.

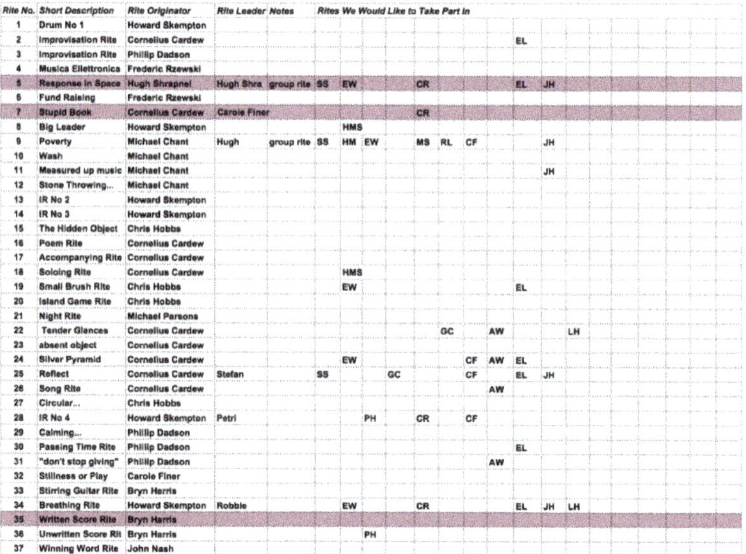

Rite No.	Short Description	Rite Originator	Rite Leader	Notes	Rites We Would Like to Take Part In										
1	Drum No 1	Howard Skempton													
2	Improvisation Rite	Cornelius Cardew											EL		
3	Improvisation Rite	Phillip Dadson													
4	Musica Ellettronica	Frederic Rzewski													
5	Response in Space	Hugh Shrapnel	Hugh Shra	group rite	SS	EW			CR				EL	JH	
6	Fund Raising	Frederic Rzewski													
7	Stupid Book	Cornelius Cardew	Carole Finer						CR						
8	Big Leader	Howard Skempton				HMS									
9	Poverty	Michael Chant	Hugh	group rite	SS	HM	EW		MS	RL	CF			JH	
10	Wash	Michael Chant													
11	Measured up music	Michael Chant												JH	
12	Stone Throwing...	Michael Chant													
13	IR No 2	Howard Skempton													
14	IR No 3	Howard Skempton													
15	The Hidden Object	Chris Hobbs													
16	Poem Rite	Cornelius Cardew													
17	Accompanying Rite	Cornelius Cardew													
18	Soloing Rite	Cornelius Cardew				HMS									
19	Small Brush Rite	Chris Hobbs				EW							EL		
20	Island Game Rite	Chris Hobbs													
21	Night Rite	Michael Parsons													
22	Tender Glances	Cornelius Cardew								GC		AW			LH
23	absent object	Cornelius Cardew													
24	Silver Pyramid	Cornelius Cardew				EW					CF	AW	EL		
25	Reflect	Cornelius Cardew	Stefan		SS			GC			CF		EL	JH	
26	Song Rite	Cornelius Cardew										AW			
27	Circular...	Chris Hobbs													
28	IR No 4	Howard Skempton	Petri				PH		CR		CF				
29	Calming...	Phillip Dadson													
30	Passing Time Rite	Phillip Dadson											EL		
31	"don't stop giving"	Phillip Dadson										AW			
32	Stillness or Play	Carole Finer													
33	Stirring Guitar Rite	Bryn Harris													
34	Breathing Rite	Howard Skempton	Robbie			EW			CR				EL	JH	LH
35	Written Score Rite	Bryn Harris													
36	Unwritten Score Rit	Bryn Harris					PH								
37	Winning Word Rite	John Nash													

Carole Finer to group (12 January 2015)

I'm on island in the middle of the Brahma Putrah river in Assam. Email obtainable about once a week. So, just to say it's good to hear from you all and I look forward to seeing you all sometime after 24th January.

152	Drum No 2	Howard Skempton													
New Rites - please add the details below then add the full description to t				here											
153	Fire from Heaven	Stefan Szczelkun													
154	Wipe Your Feet	Stefan Szczelkun			SS				CR						
155	Willy Nilly	Stefan Szczelkun			SS					GC					
156	Speak Arabic	Emmanuelle Waeckerle										AW			
157	Kiss Me	Emmanuelle Waeckerle				EW									
158	Set Strategy Rite	Les Hutchins													
159	Pop Rite	Les Hutchins								GC		AW			
160	Green Rite	Les Hutchins			SS										LH
161	NHS Rite	Hugh Shrapnel							CR						LH
162	Animal rite	Eve Libertine	EL										EL		
163	Human rite	Eve Libertine													
164	Cloud rite	Eve Libertine													
165	Meateater rite	Eve Libertine													
166	Sweet Singing	George Chambers	George							GC					
167	Naive Right	George Chambers													
168	Kiss	Ali Warner										AW			
169	Write a Rite	Ali Warner													
170	First Instrument	Ali Warner										AW		JH	
171	Asymmetry is Welco	Ali Warner	All	anytime	SS					GC		AW			
172	Exploration/Creation	Ali Warner										AW			
173	Txt rite	Stefan Szczelkun	None	anytime	SS			LH							LH
174	Cough it up rite	Bryn Harris	None	anytime											

Rite selector online spreadsheets designed by Ali Warner

Nature Study Notes Meeting (4 February 2015)

Present: Matt, Hugh, Robbie, Carole, Bron, Emmanuelle, Ali, Stefan.

We all had a chance to 'check-in' with something from our lives since we last met. This is a chance to air feelings that are on top and makes for a meeting that is not coloured by such emotions. Meetings seem to go better after a check-in, I think we all agree. (What people talk about in check-ins, especially if it is personal, should be treated as confidential.)

Duration of Performance: The duration is to be 1hr 15 mins – to a maximum of 1hr 30 mins

Use of Space: There are poor sight-lines at Cafe Oto, so we need to do raised up gestures or stand around tables which have lamps with 6" cardboard tubes attached projecting upwards. We can also have personal lights when performing. The test lamp projects a light like the moon on the ceiling, making our meeting feel like sitting around at a campsite at night. Stefan has since bought 5 more lamps from group funds. Carole will provide the cardboard tubes.

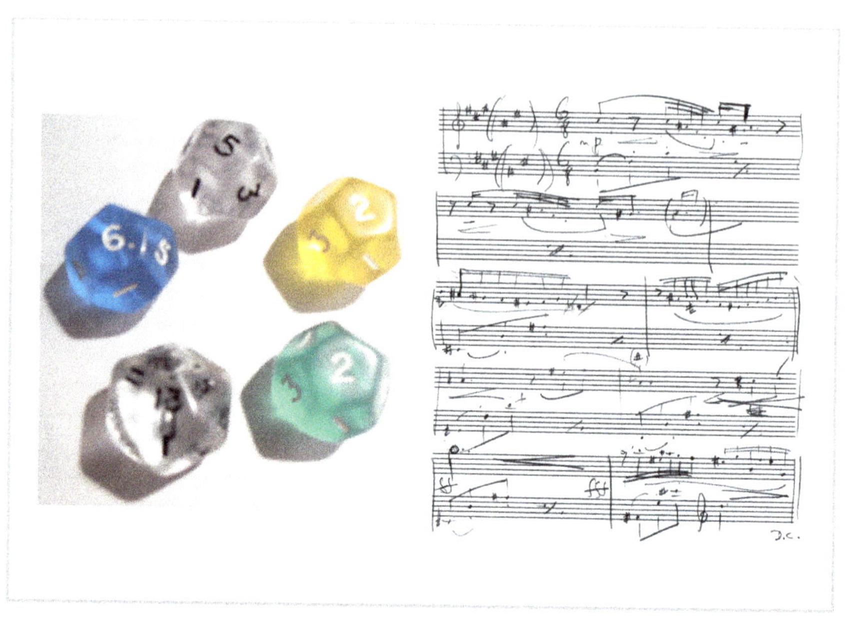

poster by Matt Scott

“I can't imagine doing the performance we did at Chisenhale at Cafe Oto, due to the lack of space” (Carole). Robbie would like to limit the amount of people that can come. Matt suggests banning one sex to halve the audience. Bron suggests banning people with beards. “We could put people (ourselves?!) behind bars” (Carole). “We can create alleyways” (Emmanuelle). “We could all stand lined up along the back wall” (Stefan).

Principles & Approach

• If there is something that you want to say or express, or an instrument you want to use, then write a rite to accommodate it or just do it - the rites should be enablers, not suppressors, of creativity (Stefan remembering his experience in the original Scratch Orchestra... rules are to be thoughtfully broken).

• A composition is where the writer specifies the sounds or dynamics to be made, usually quite definite sounds. In an improvisation rite, no sounds are specified – its more theatrical, may have more directions for the body (Hugh). A rite sets you up with a certain feeling, so that you're all improvising with the same feeling.

• We may want to be more anarchic this time.

• Exploring risk & spontaneity, beyond the normal music categories of good and bad, not wanting to review it/to assess whether we like it or not. (Robbie)

• Originally 'Scratch Music' – meant playing anything you wanted to play, but allowing for a solo to happen, thus implying that you play quietly most of the time. The solo might be you. (Carole)

• Why are we doing this? Connecting to something precious that has survived for 40-50 years. Also, some of the performances that we have seen recently have been a bit 'stuffed shirt', whereas at the time it was more unpredictable - we want to bring back the visual... the performance art feel. (Stefan)

• Is it really possible to have pure improvisation? (Robbie, on Eddie Prevost)

• The most important thing may be *feeling*... as if every sound you make is new, rather than it necessarily being the case. (Ali)

• Scratch used to include popular classics, folk tunes, Beethoven's 5th, etc. – whereas other contemporary music of the time tended to exclude melodies etc. Of course, our 'Popular Classics' may end up being hilariously funny, but no-one should play as if it were intended to be comic. (Portsmouth Sinfonia)

• We may want to write a rite. Are our rites right? What right do we have to write rites? etc. (heard by Ali)

Audience Feedback from last time

- It would have been good to have seen our organising e.g. Calling people together to perform a rite more visibly – could look at this as taking an amateur rather than professional approach. A positive value. (Robbie).

- Stefan proposed that the names of Rites are posted up around the walls. He finds the names of some of the Rites evocative/ performable. Carol disagrees. She doesn't think the Rites should be reduced to titles we give them. Ali thinks that both the full content and the symbol (title) have value and should be read carefully.

How to Start - and a discussion of a new rite by Hugh Shrapnel

- Carolyn suggested starting with Hugh's Rite no. 5 again. The group felt if would be good to start with something different.

- We talked about doing Hugh's new 'Save the NHS' Rite first. This isn't really a Rite, more agit-prop theatre. Could do it while people are queueing - a prelude. Concern is that it sets an agenda for the whole evening. Some people expressed an aversion to shouting about things that don't change. Robbie argued for the value of an abstract expression of a political feeling.

- Robbie agrees that its strange to have a direct objective within the Rites. Carole suggests doing it in the middle of the evening. Bron suggests not mentioning the NHS, although Hugh says it would no longer be the same rite. Hugh agrees it could be in the middle, or expressed through placards held up rather than shouting.

- Robbie points out that a rite (in the style of the other

rites) would say something like 'think about the NHS and act in a way that would save or destroy it'. A counter rite? Echoes of the ‘discontents’ of the earlier Scratch!

• The group has the idea that it could be done at the end as an encore. Ali said that she liked the fact that Stefan is encouraging different group members to create rites from their own passion & commitment.

• We could see that the NHS rite fits with the process of Scratch, where performances were not only rites (Robbie). The very fact of writing it has provoked this conversation, which is already interesting (Stefan). A rite may not have to be performed to be worthwhile.

• A suggestion was made that we start at Oto with Rite 9 ‘Poverty’ by Michael Chant. It needs 17 people to perform simultaneously on a piano. It is good because it *concentrates* us.

How to end

• Carol doesn't like the confusion of not knowing when to stop. Others like that aspect of improvised music. Ali asked whether we are willing risk not knowing how we are going to end - which may mean that we will also lose the power of the orchestrated ending that we had last time.

• The final singing last time was like Shaker singing - everyone belting out their song. (Carole)

Posters

• Bron will bring materials for A2-sized posters, which we can create on Sunday. One idea is that we can make posters relating to out life outside of this project on the walls at Oto – creating visual contexts for our actions.

Carol's Radio Show

- It needs to be prerecorded. Bryn can do Thursday 19th February before the concert. He could bring better recording equipment to Carol's house. We need at least 4 people at Carols for 19th February, starting at 12 noon.

Minute notes above by Ali with some additions by Stefan

Ali Warner to Stefan (10 February 2015)

I hope the notes were helpful. I just started recording the opening round of the check-in when Robbie started talking about mental health & capitalism – I thought it was a good and interesting point – but I see that the other elements that I later filled in are personal/ unique to those of us who were there!

Because I've created an open link for the Rites Selection Tracker this year i.e. people don't have to sign into a Google account, but just click on the link - to try to make it easier to access, it means that anyone who is not signed into a google account will show up as 'anonymous'!

Thanks a lot, Stefan, look forward to seeing you on Sunday.

Article on Cardew and Scratch

A feature on us written by Robert Barry. (12 February 2015)

http://daily.redbullmusicacademy.com/2015/02/cornelius-cardew-feature

Stefan: The thing that worries me is the association with Red Bull. All this talk about out music being 'wild and unruly' and 'insurgent', I can see this adding frissant to their edgy music branding of what is a really unhealthy product.

Virginia Anderson: Yes! One sees the taint of this association. Looking at the contacts for the 'education' leads to marketing and brand managers. Makes me shudder....

Stefan: As you surface from obscurity the forces of commodification start to see what profit can be made. I can remember Watney's Brewery had a slogan 'The Red Revolution' in the Sixties... I asked Robert why he was working for them and he said it was difficult to get paid well for this sort of journalism... they pay well.

PRESS RELEASE

The Scratch Orchestra's 'Nature Study Notes' at Cafe Oto on 22 February 2015

Nature Study Notes is a collection of 152 written instructions or 'scores' that was published as a booklet by Cornelius Cardew at the beginning of the Scratch Orchestra in 1969. The scores are called 'rites' and were used in many of the early Scratch Orchestra concerts. This is a music improvisation and visual performance event about one hour duration. "I must say, in hindsight, that the improvisation rites have an overall uniqueness - almost a new art form with elements of theatre, music, visuals - but amounting to something else. They have great variety (reflecting the individual character &

preoccupations of the author) but an overall character (if this makes sense!)." – Hugh Shrapnel

Performed by an ensemble of original Scratch Orchestra members and new performers including: Jane Alden, George Chambers, Linn D, Carole Finer, John Hails, Bryn Harris, Les Hutchins, Petri Huurinainen, Eve Libertine, Robbie Lockwood, Geraldine McEwan, Christian Sancto, Matt Scott, Hugh Shrapnel, Howard Slater, Stefan Szczelkun, Emmanuelle Waeckerle & Ali Warner.

"It is impossible to capture the details of such an experience in words, and of course another performance would be an entirely different experience. But this is the beauty of it." – Bachtrack

https://www.cafeoto.co.uk/events/nature-study-notes/

The pre-performance Radio Show (20 February 2015)

Carole Finer presents a weekly programme range of live music guests - from contemporary classical avant-garde to American old-time - and sometimes her own field recordings from her travels round the world. Today: Carole talks to members of the Scratch Orchestra about their latest Nature Study Notes performance taking place at Cafe Oto in two days time on Sunday February 22nd.

https://www.mixcloud.com/Resonance/sound-out-20th-february-2015/

Stefan Szczelkun to group (20 February 2015)

Very good show Carol!

Carol Finer's 'Sound Out' radio programme was excellent, with a lovely rite from Matt Scott and some interesting concise thinking from the performers. So, interesting to compare the recordings of then and now. And to hear Carol's enthusiasm for our forthcoming improvisation on the 22nd February.

The Cafe Oto performance of Nature Study Notes (22 February 2015)

Performance : Recordings and Photographs

A four track recording was made by Bryn Harris, Carol Finer and Richard Duckworth with a roving mike. The resulting mix by Richard Duckworth is extraordinary! Listen here: https://soundcloud.com/user-480336829

Photographic documentation (see below) by Deidre McGale

https://flic.kr/p/r2WNye

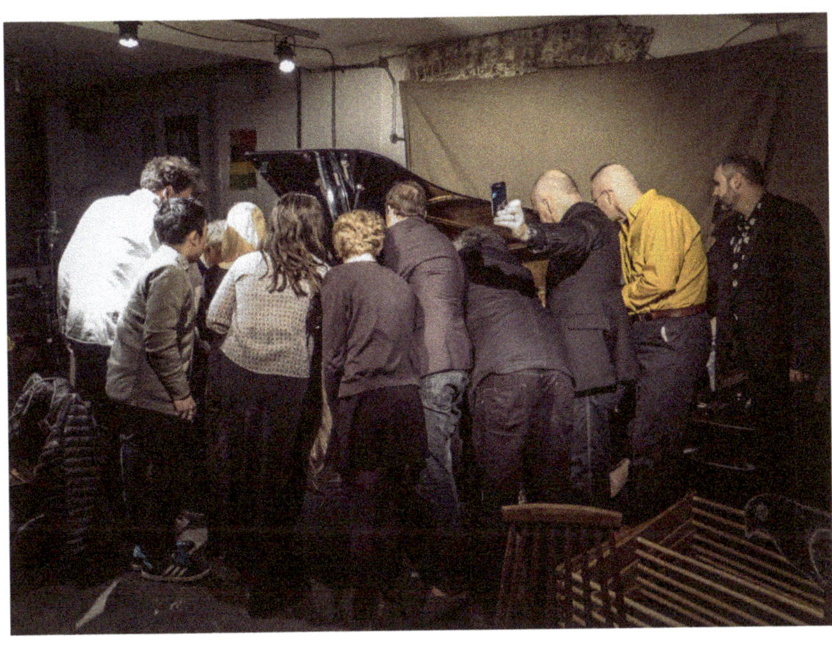

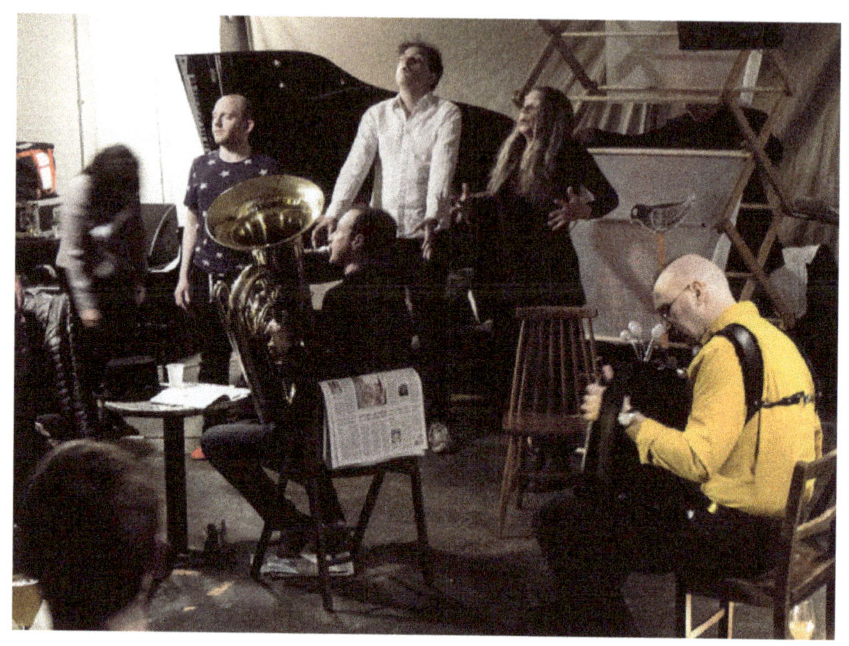

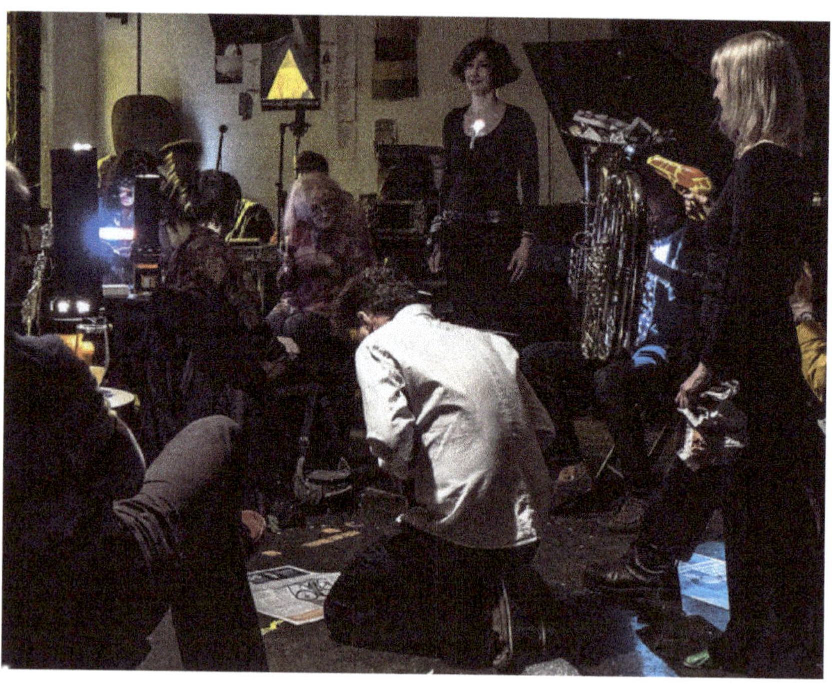

Post-performance feedback from performers

Stefan: Wonderful concert! Thanks to all of you performers! More thanks to Billy, the Cafe Oto house manager. And Deirdre McGale, who stepped in to take photographs. A very good attentive audience.

'A Dadaist scrapbook of aural and visual images' (Ali's friend). 'A winter version of our previous concert' (Jane Alden). More quotes later... I'd love to hear any favourite moments or other descriptive recollections...

John Hales: I want to write a bit more later, but one moment that really struck me was when I was standing at the back of the room playing a single note quietly on the clarinet for about 10 minutes, George Chambers started to gargle 'Jerusalem', and the soundscape around us seemed to harmonise and cohere. It was at once incredibly funny and incredibly affecting. Also, it should be said that Emmanuelle Waeckerle's 'I Love You' Rite was hilarious and a little bit disturbing. I laughed a lot more this time around but felt even more drained by the end of it! Preparing to fly back to Edinburgh now but I was thinking I might try to capture my experience in almost ethnographic form on my blog later.

http://www.napier.ac.uk/~/media/worktribe/output-175372/performingthescratchorchestrapdf

Emmanuelle Waeckerle: I feel so happy and fortunate to have been part of this. It has also proved a great cure for this lingering flu I have. Thank you all. I do hope we have more occasions to be/play/explore together with or without an audience. There are so many images and sounds in my mind... hard to pick the most memorable. First to mind is Jane Alden's beautiful medieval singing in the corner; pulling George Chambers' umbilical patriotic cord; brushing the lips of Bron Jones; Stefan's growling across the stage; Carole Chant's reading with a miner's lamp on her forehead; John Hails on all-fours under the piano. I shall soon upload a few photos taken by Howard Slater. Someone in the audience asked me afterwards. 'How do you know if it has gone well?' Good question we both thought. I pondered and replied. 'I enjoyed it and nobody walked out'.

George Chambers: My highlights were: being underneath the piano and uncomfortably having to play it, the noise was overwhelming under there!! The simplicity of the living room song with John and Jane with my eyes closed, then opening them to a swathe of gorgeous green lasers. Emmanuelle's blue lips. Robbie's live manipulation of my glockenspiel, giving me an accompaniment. Bron's confrontation with Carole re Stupid Book, and the ending which I thought was brilliant.

Ali Warner: I loved the green laser moment too. Who said it was like a Breugel?

Petri Huurinainen: Me :)

Radio post mortem

There was also a Post show discussion on Carol Finer's Sound Out show on Resonance Radio on the 6th March.

https://www.mixcloud.com/Resonance/sound-out-6th-march-2015/

Chapter 3

Archive and Evaluate

MayDay Rooms, Fleet street, London: archive and evaluate (3 May 2015)

Having been on this journey together for four years it was important to insert some traces of the work into the knowledge apparatus. The newly formed MayDay Rooms, in London's Fleet street offered a context that was conducive to the ideas.

My modest archive of Scratch papers and ephemera was lodged there and MayDay Rooms Collective offered us a day to meet and consider what we had done together. A transcription of the plenary meeting we held on 3 May 2015 is included here.

For me it was important to have a formal ending of my 'responsibilities'. I had achieved my basic aims and a lot more unexpected riches occurred on the way.

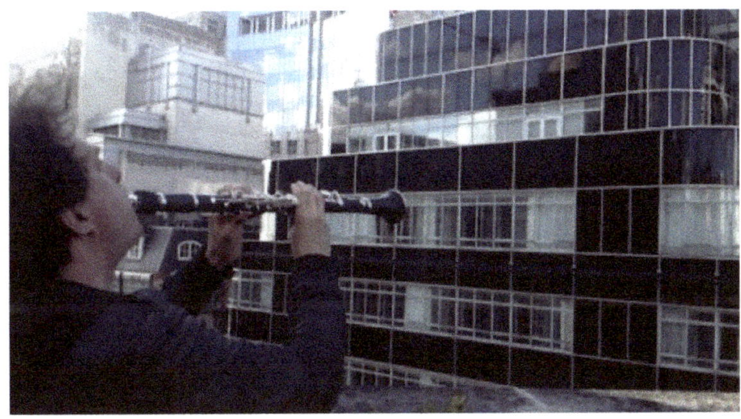

MayDay Rooms' Introduction to the event

As an initial activation of the Scratch Orchestra materials donated by Stefan Szczelkun, MayDay Rooms hosted the Nature Study Notes group. This group, comprised of ex-members of the Scratch Orchestra and interested first time participants will be convening to reflect upon a four-year project that saw them performing together many of the 'scratch rites' that were collected together in the early 1970s as 'Nature Study Notes'. The day will be a celebration of the open creative ethos and relational praxis that was the Scratch Orchestra and include post-performance reflections, documentary screenings and a perusal of archive material. Howard Slater

Nature Study Notes Group - A Reflection On Process and Performances. Transcription of a discussion.

"I must say, in hindsight, that the improvisation rites have an overall uniqueness – almost a new art form with elements of theatre, music, visuals – but amounting to something else. They have great variety (reflecting the individual character and preoccupations of the author) but an overall character (if this makes sense!)" – Hugh Shrapnel

The Nature Study Notes Group, a loose collection of former members of the Scratch Orchestra and current enthusiasts, came together, in 2013, to discuss and eventually present two performances based on the Nature Study Notes Rites (1969). The first of these performances was at Chisenhale Dance space in June 2014. This was followed by a further performance at Cafe Oto in February 2015.

The following transcript was taken from a day-long gathering of the Nature Study Notes performers at MayDay Rooms. The day included a screening of Hanne Boenisch's documentary film *'Journey to The North Pole'* (1971); a group listening to Carole Finer's Resonance Radio broadcast; a rooftop improvisation session and a forum for reflection.

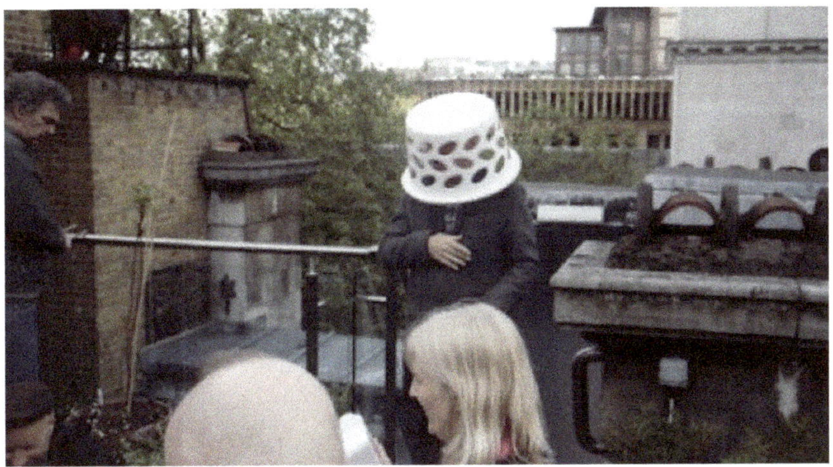

Rooftop improvisation

In the following transcript, square brackets enclose extra words or material suggested by the audio. They also provide a little extra information to assist the reader.

Michael Parsons: Well, starting with the most recent, that performance on the roof was wonderful. Very inspiring. And I felt, my immediate response was I'd rather do it that way completely without discussion than to have an improvisation rite. Which always seemed to me to be slightly awkward and artificial to have a rite to begin with. I think that if it's going to be improvisation I'd rather it was completely free; that people were responding to each other and the environment and the situation – and they don't have any allegiance to a previous text of any kind. But on the other hand looking back further I did very much enjoy the Chisenhale performance as a listener and I thought that was wonderfully lucid, transparent and inspiring. I wasn't able to get to Cafe Oto [for the second performance] certainly the Chisenhale one took me by surprise – I was expecting it to be more of a nostalgia trip, but it did actually turn out to be something really new for me.

Jane Alden: Part of the function of the Rites for me, given that not all of us have had equal experience of completely free improv, is that the Rites gave us the chance to get to know each other which is partly why what we just did on the roof was successful 'cos we do actually know each other now… it was sort of liberating to not be beholden to the Rites but the process of having used the Rites enabled that to be more productive… to do our own thing without them. I also found the Chisenhale performance very special that had something in common with that experience we just had on the roof just now, in Chisenhale we really engaged with the environment much more and our concert took place just as the light was slowly fading. There was something really magical about the birdsong being part of the performance. And I thought that was also true on the roof. And its not that… Cafe Oto is a very special venue and it was wonderful to be there but I don't feel we engaged with the environment quite as much. The way we engaged with the environment was… like a winter version of Nature Study Notes. It was an internal version, not like this evening and last June that were reaching out to the broader environment.

Linn D: Everything we've done has been special in its own way. I loved what we did at Chisenhale… I thought it was a space that responded very subtly; it had its own resonance and a special light that's been talked about, and I felt I could be delicate as well as being 'Pow!' when I felt like it. The space was receptive to that and to all of us and there was a harmony that the space generated. With Cafe Oto, it was completely different, it was just like 'get on with it!', but it was great [Laughs]

John Hails: The thing that I really love about Nature Study Notes is all that... getting on with our own little things on our own little islands, we have these invitations to go with each other, and some of us pop in and pop out of it. We've got the freedom to do it, we are not constrained to do it. I think having taken the Rites out of their original context, so that they are less ... improvisation and are something in their own right. It felt free in a lot of ways; we had these constraints but in the same way we had the freedom to use one rite here or join in with someone else's; I thought that we engaged with that in two different ways in the two different performances. That's been the very, very special part of the whole thing.

Charles Hutchins: I like the Oto performance more but that could be my own experience of it – I moved around a lot more and felt freer I guess, but it could have been [that I'd had] a bit more experience of the whole group. I've done that kind of improvisation were you just show up and shake hands with people you've never met before and get on with it. I think that's great and I like doing that. I think the Rites are a different experience than that. I didn't know them in their original context but in this new de-contextualised form... they are like improvisation but not improvisation. I think that for people who haven't done a lot of improv maybe they lead improvisation, but they don't need to do that and playing with them outside of that context has been very interesting.

Petri Hurinainen: I wasn't part of the first performance in Chisenhale. For me it was pretty much about the whole journey from the very first meeting in November 2014 to the performance in Cafe Oto and everything what happened between. The whole Scratch

Orchestra idea was opening up to me a bit by bit. It was a very pleasant change for me although I was getting a bit nervous at one point, the more I read the scorebook and the more we discussed about the Rites the more possibilities opened and I wasn't sure what to do… and then feeling totally lost before performing – I really wasn't sure - what am I going to do?! But during the performance everything started to make sense. Something clicked. It was really quite a few months journey for me… leading up to an extremely powerful moment/ experience.

Emmanuelle Waeckerle: For me it was rather the two of them and, a bit like Petri, what was really very interesting and inspiring was the whole process before the performance. Where the performance was just a release, in a way, of all these intensities generated during the discussions that happened before, between this group of very different people, with different interests and different identities, different skills, different tastes. Learning to handle all these changing energies, understandings, confusion and misunderstandings that built up throughout these meetings allowed you as an individual to find your place within the group and between yourself, the group and your own practice as well. That is what I think the Rites are for…. I use writing a lot and written scores in my own work so I relate to the Rites quite naturally but here their purpose in a way is to give us meat/matter to discuss or not and a focus for all these meetings. Whether we end up using them or not on the day of the performance doesn't really matter. Some people need them, if they haven't had much experience of improvisation for example; others don't, some need something to fight/rebel against and they can be used for that… In each performance we did, suddenly you could just be in the here and now and forget everything that happened or had been decided during the meetings. Because in the process of working out what we were going to do we had developed together as individuals and as part of the collective, and got to know each other, then comes this great release/letting go of all that, to just be in the moment.... I enjoyed the Oto performance more because it I felt maybe more comfortable, it was my second performance. I knew more of the group and I didn't feel as responsible... or self-conscious, not infringing [on others] not doing something awful... even more so being aware of the presence of some original members [of the Scratch Orchestra] in the audience and as part of the group. I felt much freer in Oto, less pressure to fit in or conform, so I enjoyed it much more. For me the big discovery is that all that work we did before in these meetings, was not about rehearsing or playing, as usually the case. It [preparation] consisted of social and verbal exchanges, absence and presence, speaking and listening, being heard and being understood, the things you agree with, and those you don't, the things you can say and the things you can't and finding ways of saying them.

Matt Scott: I was involved in the Chisenhale one and I got involved because I was curious about the idea... the famous Scratch Orchestra and what was this all about? I thought a nice way to learn about it would be to actually do some music... 'cos I was invited by another member of the group to join it. And what I suspected – and I think hasn't changed – was that the Rites were best meant as an invitation to make music, and a way of enabling a group of people... to guide them through, to liberate them to make music, rather than as an inhibition. From what I gathered, that's what the Rites function as. Rather than as dictatorial.... telling me what to play – which a normal score is – these were meant to be some kind of liberating way to get people to make music together. That depended a lot on the people involved... What amazed me was how the group respected each other's space and allowed each other's music to come out and not stamp on it, not interfere with it... It was very mutually supportive and somehow that magic happened, and I think the Rites were part of that, but also it took a big part from the group.

The two performances, Chisenhale and Oto performances – I wasn't involved in the John Cage Song Books [which the group did in 2012] – the two performances I was involved with were very different. Partly because of the environment and sound of the spaces. They were different sounding spaces, but also the fact that the audience in Chisenhale was in a line at the front of the room, with a long room going back, so we were actually more playing for ourselves, to each other, interacting with each other, which was nice because it was the first time I'd worked with all this group. In the second Cafe Oto performance, the audience were almost sitting on the 'stage' with us. We were kind of interspersed. I did wander off into the audience and had a little chat with Stefan, an improvised chat at one point which I enjoyed very much, or a nonsense chat with him doing one of the Rites at the back by the bar. But it was all part of the environment, the actual space had a big influence, so the people and the space were at least a third each of the actual outcome of the experience of the concert for me.

But the Rites really effectively worked as a sparking… as a 'kindling score' to make things happen. Especially for some people who weren't free improvisers I think. Because I've improvised freely quite a lot. And the difference between doing that, like we did upstairs [on the roof] today and playing with a score… How is it different with a score? I'm very interested in the difference it makes, whether it inhibits you, or whether it produces something magical that wouldn't happen otherwise; which I feel it did in both the performances that I was part of. So I enjoyed that.

Richard Duckworth: I'm not really a performer so much but I did end up getting shanghaied into the Cafe Oto performance, which was great actually - I really enjoyed the small part I played. And then later on I [worked on] the virtual delivery of large tracks and they had to be all synced up like a fly's eye view of the performance with a lot of different angles and perspectives, and I had to make sense of all this and reduce it to a stereo mix which I think is not the way forward. I think it should be a multi-channel mix I think it should be funked-up into a specialised surround-sound mix of some description. What came across both on the night in Cafe Oto and whilst listening to the tapes and mixing them was the fact that all the participants were excellent listeners who understood how to listen to each other and play in an ensemble. There were definitely points of divergence with people going off and doing individual parts, but then there were these wonderful points of convergence were clearly everyone is listening intently to the other people and joining towards some kind of... there was some kind of common goal there, a musical goal... or musical affect if you want to put it that way. And what was really beautiful at those points was that there was no grandstanding, nobody was showboating, there was just a lot of mutual respect and control.

Stefan Szczelkun: For me in the Oto performance I felt more confident in what I did and enjoyed my own performance more than previously... In Chisenhale I did some things where I felt "aww I wish I hadn't done that" or felt 'what was that about?' Whereas I felt confident and sometimes quite loudly confident about what I did in Oto. I don't know why, but I suddenly felt very into it and part of it as a whole. I suppose what I think about the whole thing is... How does culture work and how does a structure like that seem to get to the heart of cultural formation, rather than performing a score 'from the past' as it were? What seemed exciting about it was that it felt very contemporary. It didn't feel like we were remaking the Scratch Orchestra. Although, after Chisenhale, Hugh [Shrapnel] did say "Oh

I love Scratch Music!" as if that really was true to Scratch Music. At the same time, it didn't feel retro. I have a bad memory and a big experience was listening to Richard's mix. One of the things that comes out of listening to the 'recording', which is a very objective thing that you sit there passively not involved in all the things you are involved in when you are performing, is how much some of the Rites as compositions stand out. In particular, Carol's Rites came across very strongly and especially that last rite [using that day's] newspapers. It was like some kind of Brechtian theatre or something like that; it was very powerful. It is affecting to listen to as a recording. At first, it's quite disturbing! You think why is everyone shouting, you know, but there is something about the way it tails off into individual voices that was very good. And I also liked the engagement with the literary world through the reading and arguing that happened.

Carole Finer: Bron told me to be quiet! [Laughs]

Stefan: There were great moments of theatre that broke down [the cultural frames we use]. Was it music, theatre, art? It doesn't really matter because, somehow, it's life extruded into expression or something like that. It seemed really exciting. I'm not saying that what the people here have been saying about improvisation are not also true. I thought there were times when I was listening to the recording... and I'd be really interested to hear what other people think when you do listen to the recording. There were times... in between the group Rites when there was free improvisation, when it felt a bit like, 'this sounds like any new music improvisation'. You know, you find a space and fill it with a bit of sound and see if people respond, but when you listen to the recording of it later it's not that interesting, is it? That might be just me. Then suddenly out of that atmosphere of trepidatious exchanges there comes this very powerful moment that suddenly surges out from the recording, and you think 'my god that's amazing', kind of 'where's that come from?' It seems very new. I'm not that into 'newness' but the recording feels like it's part of today, of what's happening. That seems like the way to change the world. The way culture changes the world. When we can reinterpret what we are experiencing today in [fresh] new ways, especially in relation to each other.

Carole Finer: Chisenhale was like a Scratch concert because we shared the space with the audience and sometimes you weren't aware there even was an audience, because they were stuck at one end so you could get on with it by yourself with your people doing what you had to do. I think there was a certain amount of anarchy, that we would have had in the Scratch… but there was also mixing with others, finding another group when you knew you had to play together. You got both. I thought it was quite wonderful. And then Oto was just a bit crowded. We didn't have the space to do stuff in. You were very aware of the audience – audiences were a worry. When we had the Scratch Orchestra we often used to have more people in the Scratch than in the audience – you might have [as few as] five or six and end up with only two and they would then join in, so really you didn't worry. You have an audience at Oto and it's… you don't know if you should. I don't know, audiences are a problem. I've sometimes been at Eddie Prevost's improv workshops and you'd just get on with it. Then he'd have a Monday night at Cafe Oto and you would perform to people, and so you couldn't just be yourself and improvise. It's a bit like if you have a rite that helps you to improvise… When you've got an audience, it doesn't help you… at least it certainly makes you do it very differently. I'm not sure if that is good or bad. I don't know. Something for another time… Up on the roof [today] we weren't really worried if anyone was listening except the birds… I'm not sure what the audience gets out of it. I'm not an audience so I don't know. I sometimes think it's a big fraud [Laughs]. I don't know. [A Fraud Rite? ed.]

Robbie Lockwood: [My thought is] somewhere between Stefan and Carol because Chisenhale was surprisingly beautiful in its lightness and the spaciousness of the place. I was quite worried that it wouldn't have the performative element that I'm used to going to as a spectator and I love Oto as a space to watch music in and listen. So I was worried it would take the edge off that, but I didn't feel that was the case – it was beautiful. There was something like playing in the park about it. Which seemed really fitting. But then the Oto performance I felt actually complemented it in a way and for me it was quite nice to have a stark, night-lit performance where personally I could listen to everything a bit more. At Chisenhale I thought I was watching a lot more and at Oto I thought I was listening more. It felt like the two complemented each other.

Howard Slater: I'm a bit regretful I didn't join in for Chisenhale or hear it because I've got no comparison. I came to Oto as a spectator, became a photographer via Emmanuelle and then joined in… crossing across different things… taping stuff… taking photographs… making sounds, and I was very excited in Oto to be inside the music in a more relaxed and less pressurised way than how I've improvised before. It felt like an honour to be moving about …. So, there was this freedom of participation that people have talked about that must have been in the open relation of the group and this encouraged me to roll a bottle or make some 'moves'. I suppose what you're [looks towards Charles] talking about is the standardised moves in improvisation, like chair pulling like I saw today. Sometimes I think within a social context the standardised moves take on a different hue, because they are in a different context rather than 'this is classic free improvisation – moving a chair'. So yes, I felt very free and very privileged… excited when I played back the four little sound-snippets that I recorded. Like it's been said there were Rites between Rites or improvisations between Rites; but all these little things just all going off… so it was really dynamic that. As a listener inside the music I was very… Yeh, stimulated, very much so, yeh.

Stefan: I've got an email from John Eden who couldn't come today. He was in the audience at Oto... Stefan leaves the room to get John Eden's email.

Jane: While Stefan is out of the room and so as he won't be embarrassed, I'll say that I felt his emails were a huge part of bringing us all together; the way he summarised what happened in the meetings that not everybody could get to. This was a wonderful cohesive force. So that's actually a way in which the Rites were modernised because of the use of email and that thread that brought us all together.

Stefan: [Introduces John Eden's comments] John Eden is somebody who is very knowledgeable about noise based music… the noise scene, but also generally about other musical genres as well… British Reggae, Grime… you name it. He really gets into things. He's a respected commentator.

Carole: [Reads John's email missing his apologies for not being here]

John Eden writes: "I really enjoyed the performance at OTO. I wish I'd made some notes but essentially, I was expecting something quite serious and was very pleased to find it was a lot more varied than that. I liked the combination of both a lot going on and not much going on (often at the same time) and it was clear that the performers knew each other well enough to work together but still allow for surprises. (This is one of the main criticisms of seeing free jazz trios at Cafe OTO – it's great but you do wonder exactly how surprising someone can be with sax, bass, drums in 2015). It also felt like a space that was both gloriously and depressingly out of step with neoliberalism, if that isn't being too pretentious. "No Stars Here" as they used to say about the 'Dead by Dawn' parties."[121 Railton Road, 1994-96]

Matt: "No Star!?" Is that his rating!? [Laughter]

Michael: I took that as a complement. [Others chip in] "No egos... yeh, yeh"

Michael: Not only that but no star rating is also non-judgemental.

Discussion is opened to the floor:

Emmanuelle: At Oto talking about the audience, Martin Pover a friend who was in the audience who goes to a lot of improv concerts, asked that question: He said 'How was it? I said 'Great, I enjoyed it'. He said: 'How do you know such a performance was a success or not? How do you judge it?'

Carole F: Interjects: They did clap a lot!?

Emmanuelle: Yes, but I thought that was a good question because ... the audience don't know Nature Study Notes or the structure behind what happened. He said 'Not that that was necessary to appreciate it', but knowing what it is about kind of helps. 'How do you judge the quality, the value of it?' My only answer was that, 'Well I enjoyed it and nobody walked out'. [To Carol] You said that you had 5 or 6 people with 2 left...

Carole: People walked out, but they would also be insulting as they walked out! I'm thinking of the concert 'Beethoven's Today' at the South Bank.

Michael: They demanded their money back didn't they. They thought it was going to be a proper Beethoven concert. [Laughter and chat]

Stefan: For new people, what was it like today to see the documentary [Of the Scratch Orchestra] in terms of what we've done? It's quite a rare documentary not very often seen. Was it just like 'oh yeh that's what we've been doing... no surprises'. Or was it like 'eh?'

Jane: I learned a lot from seeing that footage. Particularly the recognition by the original [members] that they weren't engaging with working people on a daily basis and therefore there was this discussion or need for discussion about how to reach working people. That was really revealing to me.

Emmanuelle: I had seen footage before in an exhibition but not this footage. That was before taking part, when I did the Great Learning. But now in retrospect looking... and comparing with us, I thought they were, or you were (addressing the original Scratch Orchestra members present) much more tactile and much more physical in a way... I felt that all of us were.... Interacting, yes with sound and things, but there was a much more tactile quality to the extracts we saw. I'm not sure if 'tactile' is the right word but physical.

Linn D: [Affirms] Physical, because there's space to perform, you are using your whole being and not just your voice or body, but with expression and movement and theatre, so I don't ever think of Scratch Music, of Nature Study Notes, as music. It was interesting to hear what you said Matt, because I never think of it as music, I think of it as doing things, or as performance and interaction with any bit of creativity that happens to fit in at the time it happens. If you thought 'I might use this prop in this bit' or something... There is a gorgeous freedom to... play. For me it's 'play'. Like children play.

Petri: I've done just one performance with Scratch Orchestra but comparing to the documentary we saw earlier, as Emmanuelle says, it was much more physical. I'm thinking if we do perform again, say five performances, then each performance is going to be different and probably will evolve in different directions and various things could happen. Comparing what we've done now on the roof to the previous one [Oto] in which there was more going on, it was more active. Things will happen and change when we play again.

Stefan: One very similar thing about the Village Concerts [in the documentary] was that they were self-organised and very cheaply done because we were camping and nobody was paid, but there were no big costs involved. So, everyone just paid for themselves to camp, and then we went into these village halls which had somehow been set up but were not proper music venues. Our limitation now is that if we wanted to perform in Dublin or the Huddersfield New Music Festival, even if we got invited to something like that, it would suddenly cost £10,000 plus to put the thing on. All the people we've had working for nothing, including photographers, reviewers etc. I mean we had 17 people... if each of us was getting a standard £500 artist's fee plus travel and accommodation, it's a lot of costs. So, we did achieve something in those village concerts [in the early 70s] .... unlike the Queen Elisabeth Hall or the Beethoven Today concerts or some of the other London music venues... We were outside of the Music scene, we were doing something 'out of context'. [Recently] we were playing Cafe Oto which is a recognised place [for experimental music] but we were unfunded and, even here we are completely outside of the establishments invitations, validation or opprobrium? I don't even know what that word means? [Laughter] John: You've written a whole piece about the Chisenhale thing. Did what you experience at Oto or saw today change you thinking?

John: No, not really, it was just another example of these little communities bubbling up and then evaporating. I'd agree with people saying there was more freedom in the second performance because I'd had the experience of seeing it once. My experience of the whole thing has been a little bit different because I've not been able to come to many meetings being up in Edinburgh. So for the first performance I deliberately selected Rites where I could just parachute in and perform. And then I found myself regretting that I wasn't sufficiently prepared in the other Rites, so I couldn't just step in and take part in someone else's Rite. So, for the second performance I'd done a lot more preparation in terms of making myself more flexible in terms of what I could do and what I couldn't do which built on that... Interesting watching that documentary – it was showing that similar kinds of activity, but in a completely different historical setting, can result in something completely different. Although... we can relate the processes to each other. It was seeing a very different political backdrop and I don't think... it wouldn't have been authentic for us to perform like those late 60s early 70s Scratch Orchestra performances now because things have changed. We are different, media is different, it's a very, very different set-up and we've responded in what I think – if we can use such a term – an authentic way to us. I think that is really valuable.

Howard: I think something along the lines that a relationship can have a sound. Or a social relation can have a sound. While I think there was this certain historical context when I watched that footage again I saw punk on its way – people just bashing instruments and things like that. I don't think you could claim that Scratch Orchestra was a harbinger of punk music, but there is a similar sort of... Roger Sutherland uses the word – 'amorphousness' to describe the Scratch sound and that chimed with what I was hearing at Oto. So that sort of sense of just a freedom-to-be. And all punk groups were a form of relationship – I was in punk groups. You couldn't just get together one-off, you had to be friends... there was a sort of social relationship it was based on. If anything, to link trans-historically, it's that sense of a relationship that allows people to just sit there and click their fingers. Or in some of the footage where three people are sat in a row. And I always dreamed that this scratch approach to music could become like punk began... The Fall said "let's get this thing together and make it bad" on one of their tracks from the 'Dragnet' LP. Good/bad, but, you know what I mean. That kind of ethos was in punk. What people don't expect from music or professional musicians – shitness, you know the wonderful sound of shit!

John: Arte Povera? A Poor Art...

Les: What struck me about you guys back in the day was how boundlessly optimistic it was [laughter]. I really dislike the word 'authenticity' so I'm not going into that. I don't think you can be boundlessly optimistic like that these days, because it doesn't seem like the world is changing in a direction that is necessarily going to benefit everyone involved these days, but then I have the sense that what you guys felt like what you were doing was making the world better and more meaningful, if not for a larger society at least for you personally. The total disrespect for stupid questions from the interviewer [in the documentary] was like 'I don't care that I'm gonna pull out grass from the ground' [rather than answer]. That guy (was he from the Daily Mirror?)... Seeing the responses to him... [from Cornelius Cardew's slowed down language and Stefan's swinging silver disc]. Was there no reporting? ... It [showed] such confidence. And the other thing that struck me was how completely 'out' it was. The string rite I recognised people doing, and I know someone did that at Oto and they tied yarn around themselves and stuff – it was true to the words [of the rite] – but what you guys did with it back then when you were tied together and practically unable to move! ... Everything was pushed as far as it could go. In our next performance, I'm gonna be looking at how far things can be pushed, rather than what is specifically true to what's written, but what can we do with what's written that takes it all the way, or as far as it can go. I think that was really interesting.

Loud vocal affirmative responses.

Howard: I think that what Stef got into about the Village Concerts and that footage [we saw] is that some of the people in the original Scratch Orchestra were 'out there', like in the Richmond Park Journey. Actually, doing it outside, I think that would be good thing to do next. Like in a park or something. I like that idea of troubadours.

Carole: Yeh, that brings to mind that Michael Parsons did an outdoors performance which you [turns to Michael] did around Canary Wharf only a couple of years ago. I followed them with a microphone. It was wind instruments having to play to constructions, to do with the buildings.

Michael: [Interjects] It was all brass instruments in fact and it was to do with evoking echoes from the glass surfaces. That was like being outdoors – you had to get permission but – then you were just let loose; there was a lovely freedom in doing that. Passers-by stopping and not really understanding but stopping and listening. I think they enjoyed it. Nice to do an outdoor one, yeh.

Emmanuelle: What I'm going back to, when I say I want to find the right words... When I said 'physical' before – the difference between then and now – so it's not physical, it's more radical and raw. When I saw that [in the documentary] I was questioning 'so how come we were not?' There's all reasons... and we are quite radical people in our way and have done things which are pretty out there with our works individually. Is that because there is less a need? I would have never thought to go and perform naked like that blond woman [Bergit Burkhardt] in that long transparent dress. Because I felt it wouldn't be relevant now or needed. Perhaps it's about something else? But I was really impressed. What triggered that was seeing the tied-up rite as well. I thought 'Yes!', seriously tied up! Really, really. It becomes close to bondage. So, the question is ... is it a different way of radicalism? Or is it, because we know, we are so aware of what has been done and there is this kind of revisiting and making it contemporary again?

Les: I think a lot of improvisation has become kind of codified. Part of the reason I'm able to go up in groups who've never met before and free-improvise with them is because we all know what is expected. When you were inventing... [those codes?] you didn't know what was expected. I think that rediscovering the unexpected would be a great way forward.

Robbie: For me a lot of this touches on it... I find it hard to speak after that. Something about touch is very present there. There is a world that I've grown up in that is corporate London which means you don't personally [engage] – this is my experience of it – there is the feeling of always being followed by CCTV. There is a feeling that, while you may not feel you are doing something wrong, but still you check yourself. Even then you're not sure. So, there is something about Scratch that is I think crucial, I think it's tentative, and I think it's about saying, 'we dare to step outside'. We dare to go to places we haven't previously determined. There is something there about the collective and the sensible. There is something about the sensible and empathy which is in trouble today. And it comes with that kind of paranoiac attitude we've got in the City of London. I think it needs to be challenged from every single angle. Scratch is one small attempt to prick that bubble. And I felt that. And personally… to say something of my experience. I made a sound on my guitar that I'd never made before. That is something new to me. I was excited by that. It was the kind of thing that I would have been a bit too inhibited to do in other kinds of performances. So, it's something about the relation and the sensible there. It wasn't really obvious to anyone else, I didn't go and hug anyone or anything like that. But it made a little imprint in my own world that gave me some confidence, that gave me a playing and listening experience which was significant.

Quiet pause

Jane: Linn talked about play and whether or not this was music. And firstly, I would like to say that I think that it absolutely is all music, and music includes play but it seemed watching the footage that … I was surprised when Cornelius Cardew said it was apolitical. It seemed that that was more about play in a sense than what we've been doing recently. There's a political agenda just in the very fact of doing this now. There is more of an awareness (as Robbie was saying) of our relationship to this cultural moment in time than just the fact we are wanting to revisit some of these ideas or see what it means to bring these people together. I had exactly the same experience that Robbie just described of feeling liberated that I wouldn't do in other artistic contexts – that I wouldn't have felt enabled to do and that is something that is very politically empowering at a kind of local level that can be empowering in a larger sphere as well. So, in that sense it's not so much about play it's actually about something that is very real.

Linn D: I also think that not knowing what to do, not knowing how to respond, was a very important part of doing things in the old days as well as now. 'Cos, I haven't a clue; I could do anything or nothing'. Or something very, very, very small. And bewilderment for me was part of it and in a sense, it still is, even though I might have a few more tools these days that I can use and a better idea. I quite like the 'not knowing' as much as the knowing and the feeling of 'Oh my god. I don't know how to tackle this' and then stay with that and use it, and empty my mind and then... something will come. I don't like to use my mind I want to use the un-mind.

John: I want to pick up on the idea of play as not to do with the real world. One of the lessons I think I get from this is that we need more play in the real world. That we discover things we didn't know and the idea that we don't have or feel we have the permission, or whatever, to actually try things out means that we take the safe option. We go down the route that we know will not land us on the street or... I think [this kind of play] does encourage you to take risks because beautiful things happen when you take risks.

Jane: It's hard, [now, to believe] what you said about the village halls that allowed you to perform. I mean that is unbelievable and could not happen now. I mean they took a risk those village halls – they had no idea what you were going to do and they were willing to just open their doors and just see what happened.

Stefan: [Interjects] I'm not sure it was like that actually... I think they might have been hired.

Carole: [Adds] I went and got them and they didn't really ask what we wanted them for [laughter] and we didn't have to pay very much money. They didn't seem to mind.

Matt: It seems like there were only two people there anyway! [Laughter].

Carole: When we performed at the Purcell Room or somewhere where Catherine went through the audience... It was Beethoven Today. She forgot he was meant to be deaf and thought he was blind, and so she went around the audience with a blindfold on! Blundering her way up the aisles through the audience. The ushers would have made her sit down now. Things – in proper halls – you could never do now.

Jane: I mean the work that Stefan had to do to get us Cafe Oto. That was a tremendous amount of work.

Carole: You didn't have to say exactly what we were going to do did you?

Stefan: That is complex because first I got it for Songbooks in the year of Cage's anniversary; there was a strong connection with Resonance which Carol and I are close to. It took a long time but that was just getting busy people to respond to emails.

Carol: I do think we all like what we're doing. We've all enjoyed what we did. The freedom that people have talked about. Freedom of expression. Being free individually and collaborating, I think that is all very positive. I think maybe I should not be worried about the audience either, because really when the audience come they seem delighted, don't they... I know someone who comes to improvisation things - he didn't come to our performance – and he has his eyes shut the whole time. Well, if you were playing you would think 'Oh he's fallen asleep', but actually that is how he listens, so even if you had your eyes shut in Cafe Oto, you were probably listening.

Stefan announces the imminent end of recording but asks for final comments.

John: We talked about not forcing things, not making them happen. One thing that was very valuable about the whole process while we're looking at Nature Study Notes was how although... we talked about the whole thing being led by Stefan, I think that the way that you've [turns to Stefan] avoided leading it. The way that you've avoided making it easy for us. It's actually been an effective way of dealing with the whole thing. There were various moments where it looked like some people wanted something a bit more strict, they wanted to be able to slot in. And those were somehow evaded and that it all happened because it was self-organising in a lot of ways. The hard work you put in that Jane's already talked about to establish the infrastructure of the performance and things like that. But actually, there was lots of hard work, as well as not leading it. [Laughter]

Stefan: Thank you for any complimentary aspects of that but it's part of the ethos of the whole thing you know. It would have been weird to do it another way. In fact, one of the things that drove me originally with the Songbooks particularly was the fact that the performances I was seeing, e.g. by Exaudi, were so uptight and I just thought that they'd completely lost the original anarchic visual and unpredictable quality of those performances and I wanted to bring that back. Being a visual artist [active at the time] I knew what had been lost from some of those things that had been revived. And I thought we brought that back successfully. Just to finish I would like to make an admission. Projects like this, in my older age, I look at as an operation on culture. They are a kinda' surgical – well it would be horrible to do this to a real person because it would be totally messy and they'd lose bits of their body... It's surgical in the sense that I'm strategically trying to think of ways to operate on culture. This thing of being inter-generational and playing around with scratch knowledge and bringing all those things together. In the longer-term I was influenced by Howard's thinking and writing as well, and the relationships that have come into it. Robbie and Ali [not here today] have been a very important part of the younger group members. So, for me today has been a wonderful and unbelievable thing that we can have this non/anti-institution to host a space to reflect on what we've been doing. That is something I've never experienced before in my life. I was never able to benefit from the counter culture of the Sixties on that level [thinking of the Arts Lab, Drury Lane.] To me it's all come together in a very extraordinary way and I'd like to thank you all here for the contributions you've made to this. You have made an exploration of the past, that could have been dry or academic, extremely rich and going beyond anything I could have imagined at the beginning of it. To me it's been a wonderful process. I don't know what the effect of this 'surgery' really is! But it seems that there is a lot of good will or 'vibes' from the 60s and 70s that are being channeled into the current time in some kind of weird way that culture works. Yah!! But what happens next is open. For me the project has ended.

Carole: You can't just leave us alone! [Laughter]

Stefan: You've all grown up now you've gotta leave home!

Transcription by Stefan Szczelkun & Howard Slater - 15/5/2015 & 9/1/2018

http://maydayrooms.org/event/scratch-orchestra-activation-nature-study-group/

Chapter 4

Documenta 14 in Athens 2017

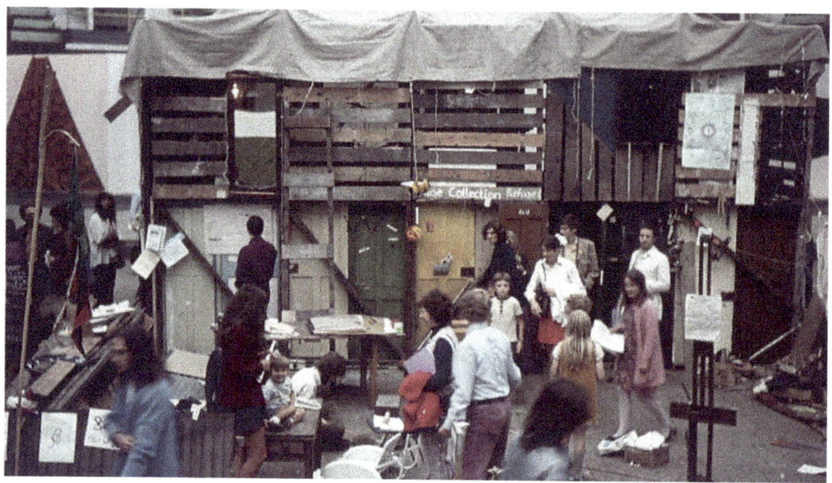

The Scratch Cottage - Art Spectrum, London 1971 photo by Walerian Szczelkun

Nature Study Notes - intensified and exported

1. Through the research of curator Pierre Bal Blanc, Carol and I were invited to activate the Scratch Orchestra archive material that was being shown at Documenta 14. This was part of a wider focus on the works of Cornelius Cardew.

2. We got to work with a new group much less selected than the London players. This was open to all in the same way the Scratch Orchestra was in 1969. The process of

preparation was compressed into three days of 4 hour workshops.

3. There are also some thoughts on what it means to export such a cultural phenomenon in the context of Documenta 14 in Athens, Greece.

4. The workshops were in a large space along with the Scratch Orchestra archival exhibits.

Three open improvisation workshops in Documenta 14, Athens, Odeion Athinon, 2 - 6pm on 3, 4 & 5 May 2017.

Introduction

The workshops were run by Carole Finer and myself, Stefan Szczelkun. We were both members of the Scratch Orchestra 1969 - 1974 and the workshops were mainly based on a founding text of the Scratch Orchestra, entitled 'Nature Study Notes'. This is a collection of 152 written instructions or rites compiled by Cornelius Cardew from his composition classes at Morely College. The rites were described by Cardew in the 'draft constitution':

"Members should constantly bear in mind the possibility of contributing new rites. An improvisation rite is not a musical composition; it does not attempt to influence the music that will be played; at most it may establish a community of feeling, or a communal starting point, through ritual." A Scratch Orchestra: draft constitution. June 1969.

The workshops were in a large exhibition space in the basement of the Odeion Athinon. The Athens Music Academy is on the upper two floors. Before giving an account of what we did I am going to talk briefly about an older thought that was resurrected in me by this event.

Doing these three days of intensive workshops I realised that whilst in the Scratch Orchestra I had had the idea that rites could be a widespread practice that might be able to renew human cultural activity. This means that although the Nature Study Notes are a beautiful historical collection, this way of working can be enacted by any group of people anywhere in the world who are wanting to remake or revolutionise cultural practices. The process of rite writing can also grow with political consciousness.

After my first use of the rites in the early Seventies I researched basic human ability doing a lot of dance and bodywork classes over a period of several years. I made a collection of about 200 'exercises' by which anyone can experience a full range of elemental human abilities. Our senses pick-up environmental data which is stored and evaluated in our brains which can then result in physical action. The collection was published as *Sense-Think-Act* and is now available as a free ebook with my original drawings. http://payhip.com/b/3TKf

What I realised in Athens was that the 'Sense-Think-Act' collection gives a schema by which a new rite praxis could utilise the full range of human expressive abilities. If the power of live culture is a continual evaluation of our conditions in all sense media, then rites could be starting places that conjoin individual and collective desires. This suggests the collapse of separated bourgeois art categories into a collective performative process.

OK! back to what we actually did in Athens.

An account of the workshops and performance

DAY 1. About 15 people turned up to take part with another 15 or so watching. Most of these people were young adults and two people had worked with the 'Nature Study Notes' rites a few weeks ago with Ali Warner. Ali had led workshops with the Documenta education teams in Athens and Kassel and had an in-depth knowledge of our way of working from being a long-term member of the London performing group documented earlier.

After a round of introductions and physical warm-up exercises. We started with 'Rite 5' by Hugh Shrapnel:

HMS 5 Improvisation Rite. (This is an abridged version as found in NSN notes) 'Any number of people making any sounds. Perform in a large area, as widely separated from each other as possible. Performers stay in the same place throughout, keeping physical movement to a minimum.'

This requires a lot of listening, only using your body to produce sounds and a minimum of movement. We found it to be a good starting place before. After performing the rite we had a feedback session so people could say something about what they had experienced. Several people thought it was a beautiful experience.

Photocopies of Nature Study Notes had been made by Lou Forster, a D14 worker, and these were now handed-out and people asked to choose one or two of the 152 rites. We read out these choices and then chose two rites to perform. The person who selected it was asked if they would like to lead. The chosen rites were the 'Giving Rite' by Phillip Dadson and one by Cornelius Cardew that was more difficult.

Rite PD 31 'If you have something to give, give it. Don't hesitate to give, yet choose the time or space. If you have nothing to give, receive. By receiving you are under no obligation to give, yet it is better to give than receive. Stop making music when you please, but don't stop giving.'

Rite CC67 (Men) Discover a rhythm external to you. Bring it to light. Establish it. (Men) Take an idea which you are normally totally indifferent to and believe in it passionately. (Women) Disregard the evidence of your senses.

We discussed both improvisations immediately after doing them. The 'Giving Rite' produced a loving intensity amongst the players with much use of touch. It was a good choice as it quickly brought the group close together. The second rite challenged us conceptually.

After a break, we sat down for a relatively formal discussion of improvisation. Carole and I made connections to issues that arose in the Scratch Orchestra and especially to things that contributed to the politicisation of the group from c1972 and eventually the halting of the 'Nature Study Notes' style of improvisation. Our curator Pierre Bal Blanc took part in these discussions and spoke at some length. Others were also eloquent, in particular Mika who had worked Ali Warner.

A list of topics covered in our first discussion.

- Listening and playing in response to others as against improvisation by listening to one's inner impulses.

- Playing as an accompaniment to other people, or playing a solo. "An accompaniment is defined as music that allows a solo (in the event of one occurring) to be appreciated as such." Cornelius

Cardew, draft constitution, 1969

• Rite or composition? A composition tells the player to do something, but a rite simple sets a shared mind-set or metaphor for an improvising action.

• Who are we playing for, an audience or for ourselves? Relating back to the widespread use of the slogan 'Art for Whom' in the Sixties. This was the title of a Serpentine Gallery exhibition in 1978 and as Carole pointed out was originally a quote from Mao Tse-tung, from his 'Talks at the Yenan Forum on Literature and Art', 1942. It's in the conclusion, paragraph 1. "The first problem is: Literature and art for whom?"

• Explicit meaning or intuitive expression? Spontaneity, unpredictability and live discovery or controlled programming? This issue was related to the 1971 - 74 'Discontents' of the Scratch Orchestra in which explicit and ideologically 'correct' meaning came to be favoured.

• Skill, practice and virtuosity versus artless sensitivity and openness. One tending to become exclusive and the other tending to be more inclusive.

Participants were invited to come to Frederic Rzewski's piano concert the following evening at the Megaron. The concert was titled 'The People United Will Never Be Defeated'. We were all offered free tickets.

DAY 2. Introductions were made again as there were new players with some people from yesterday unable to attend. We started with a warm up led by Stathis Grafanakis who had theatre experience. The people who had come to yesterday were invited to tell new people what to expect. We began with a rite that had been chosen yesterday followed by a discussion. This was Rite BG 63 by Bob Guy. 'The group chooses a suitable outdoor site and waits for rain. Meanwhile improvisation take place in an attempt to induce rainfall.'

We then had an hour-long formal discussion. The first half hour was spent with Carole and I talking about our memories and thoughts about the Scratch Orchestra's 'Discontents' from 1971, which had led to a large part of the group, including Cornelius Cardew, becoming Marxist-Leninist revolutionaries. Improvisation, as exemplified by the Nature Study Notes' rites, then came to be seen as reactionary. This eventually led the orchestra becoming inactive in its original open form. Cardew made efforts for some years to restructure the group to toe the party line. Carole had been part of the Discontents meetings and subsequent politicisation, whilst Stefan, although he had been political before this, was doing other things at this point in time.

The second half of the discussion tried to switch attention to any current 'discontents' in Athens, and in particular, in relation to Documenta in Athens. This was somewhat uncomfortable as the curator and his assistant were present and active in discussion. I spoke about how the level of hospitality we had received made it difficult to 'bite the hand that feeds us'. My own main criticism of D14 would have been something in relation to Art canon formation. I had just been reading 'Partisan Canons' ed. by Anna Brzyski (Duke UP 2007). But I was not ready to mount even a concise critique. Later on, one of the curators left and two Athenians did speak. However, as it turned out there was little or no animosity expressed towards D14. The issue of the payment of invigilators, which had been a bone of contention, had been resolved with a compromise settlement reached. The issue of the involvement of Athens-based artists was acknowledged but not seen as having a structural iniquity. The issue of D14 not supporting the squat movement, which has been fighting evictions recently, did not come up in this discussion. (I later painted two placards: 'CLOSE THE CAMPS NOT THE SQUATS' and 'CEASE WAR ON GRASSROOTS INITIATIVES' but did not hear of a reaction to them.)

After this we brought out a box of small cakes and gave them out to the players. People dispersed for a half-hour break. To end the day, we did two more rites. The first one was a rite written by Carole Finer that I chose:

Rite CF146 'Page one of the Evening Standard current on the day of the performance. Each performer has a copy which he will use as his score. Performers decide individually how they wish to interpret the score and perform accordingly for a given length of time.'

For this we used Greek newspapers that were procured by Lou Forster. (who had been great at supplying anything we needed throughout our time there.) After this very focused and somewhat dense rite we tried to make things more complex by performing three rites, chosen by the participants, simultaneously!

Rite MP21 by Michael Parsons. 'Place comfortable mattresses about the room. Those who feel tired lie down. The others play or sing relaxing music. A player who is tired may also lie down. Ends when any or all of those lying down are asleep…'

Rite HS55 by Howard Skempton. 'Drop everything. Do it gently for fear of damage.'

Rite BH93 by Bryn Harris. 'Play in a circular fashion. Increase the diameter of the circle. The music should finally be ingested by its own fundamental orifice.'

Michael Parson's 'lying down' rite contrasted dramatically

with Howard Skempton's 'Dropping things'. This was a very satisfying fifteen minutes of structured chaos. It gave people a taste of what the performance tomorrow might turn out like with a more complex layering of activity.

Before everyone dispersed at 6pm we reminded people of our performance at 5pm the next day. We introduced 'The Stupid Book rite' by Cardew and asked people to bring their own choice of a 'stupid' book. We also asked participants to write new rites! "Any suggested rite will be given a trial run and thereafter left to look after itself." Cornelius Cardew, A Scratch Orchestra: draft constitution. 1969.

Rite CC7 'Take a stupid book. A reader reads aloud from it while the rest improvise. The role of the reader may wander, a) through the reader presenting the stupid book to someone else, and b) by someone wresting the stupid book from the reader. A reader may attempt to terminate proceedings by ceasing to read aloud from the stupid book.'

DAY 3. The public performance starting at 5pm was to include the rites we had done on previous days plus any new rites that people had written. We started this day with a discussion of the Scratch Cottage. This was a disorderly structure built by members of the Scratch Orchestra for a major art exhibition in London in 1971. Archive material borrowed from Mayday Rooms in London was displayed in a three metre long vitrine to the rear of the space we were using. The Scratch Cottage, as exhibited at Art Spectrum, London 1971, was first conceived by myself, Stefan Szczelkun, as a place to perform Scratch Music - insulated from the high art context.

My idea was to challenge the often classically trained musicians to construct a shelter with their own hands. The materials were recycled rough floor joists and old doors. Each musician or small group made a structural frame using the simplest of hand-tools: hammers, saws and nails. The frames were then bolted together to make a simple enclosure.

It countered fine art aesthetics with a basic level of material engagement. At the same time, it referenced my research into self-built vernacular housing - the UK Plotland movement.

The players had not arrived at 2pm, but because of the upcoming performance we had to begin our discussion of the Cottage without them. In fact, performers did arrive as Carole and I were gathered around the vitrine discussing the Scratch Cottage with some passing exhibition visitors.

We then did a warm-up for the players followed by a discussion about the concert. No-one had thought about how to structure it so, as I had been thinking about his overnight, I proposed a plan. My plan suggested starting with the performance of two consecutive rites and then going into doing the simultaneous rites we had done the day before. This was to be followed by new rites written by the players. Happily, Eleni and Mika had written some new rites so they read out their rites. Eleni had written several rites and so the group voted on which ones to perform.

New rites by Helen 'Eleni' Zervou:

EZ 1. Protest against the creator of the rite/ against the rite itself. Create a "procession"/ demonstration/ riot to express your opposition.

EZ 2. Take a very important decision collectively or individually. Then do the opposite to what you have decided.

EZ 3. Express your gratitude to the institution (if there isn't one, then make it up).

EZ 4. Breathe collectively.

EZ 5. Everybody in the room uses their voice to sing a single continuous note, different than the ones sung by the people around them. The same note cannot be sung by two people. As an interval do the reverse (everybody sings the same note).

EZ 6. Act Normal.

EZ 7. Be the audience.

The players chose to perform numbers EZ 4 and EZ 6.

New rite by Mika Ebbsen:

Performers move through a space. Everyone is walking/moving towards the doorsteps of change. When the performer finds his/her door, stop. Performers can only make a sound with a singular quality of any duration in lieu of knocking on this metaphorical door. The noises made must correspond to each performer's emotions vis à vis their desires for change. 1) Wait for the right moment to knock. 2) Knock right away and wait for a reply. The performance ends once everyone has knocked and feels satisfied to leave the unanswered door or feels a response emerged and walks through the door. It is not permitted to stay waiting forever.

We decided not to rehearse Mika's rite, after some discussion, as it needed to be fresh and unrehearsed.

Carole and I had decided to end the performance with a rite that we had used to end one of our London concerts. This was to get everyone to line up and simultaneously sing their 'favourite' song loudly at the audience. (Based on Rite CC 26 'Sing a song in unison.')

The Stupid book rite (I think 4 people had brought stupid books) was to be done 'as and when' people judged it was the right time.

The group then tried out Eleni's rites in two groups. One group that had the label 'female', did the 'Breathe Collectively' rite whilst the other group, labelled 'male', did the 'Be Normal' rite. These trials went well.

We then had a break to arrive back for the performance at 5pm sharp! We were pleased to see that there were 18 people who had turned up to perform. (Our curator Pierre Bal Blanc and Lou Forster who had taken part in some of the workshops, did not participate in the final performance)

One person had sketched out a programme that was copied along with a list of most of the performers: Petros Chytiris, Alexandra Damiragi, Mika Ebbsen, Maria Gouveli, Stathis Grafanakis, Kai Hansen, Achilleas Karagiannidis, Sarris Ioannis, Thodoris Pistiolas, Kassapis Andreas Ragnar, Janna Mirl Redmann, Marina Stavrou, Barbara Voltea, Helen 'Eleni' Zervou.

The performance began on time and proceeded until we ended with the individual songs all begun at the same time. It all seemed remarkable coherent and I heard someone in the audience say they found it 'moving'. However, it is difficult to judge the quality of a performance from within it!

Carole and I then pinned small bells hanging from red ribbon onto the players to thank them individually before we dispersed. We made a special public thanks to our curator Pierre Bal Blanc, who had made it all possible.

Later on, back in London, Carol edited the audio she recorded and we made a radio programme with it. In it you can hear some audio samples of the concert as well as excerpts from the discussions.

https://www.mixcloud.com/Resonance/sound-out-11th-july-2017/

Photo-documentation of the Athens performance by Stathis Mamalakis

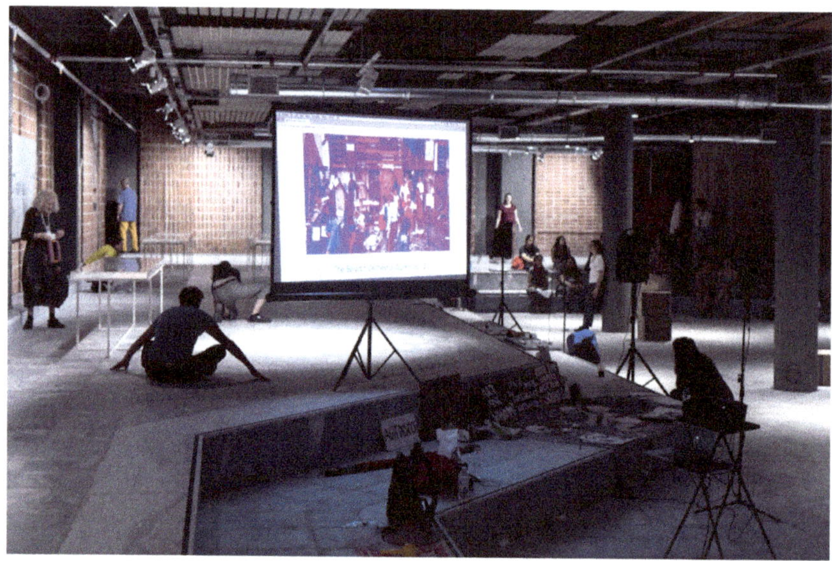

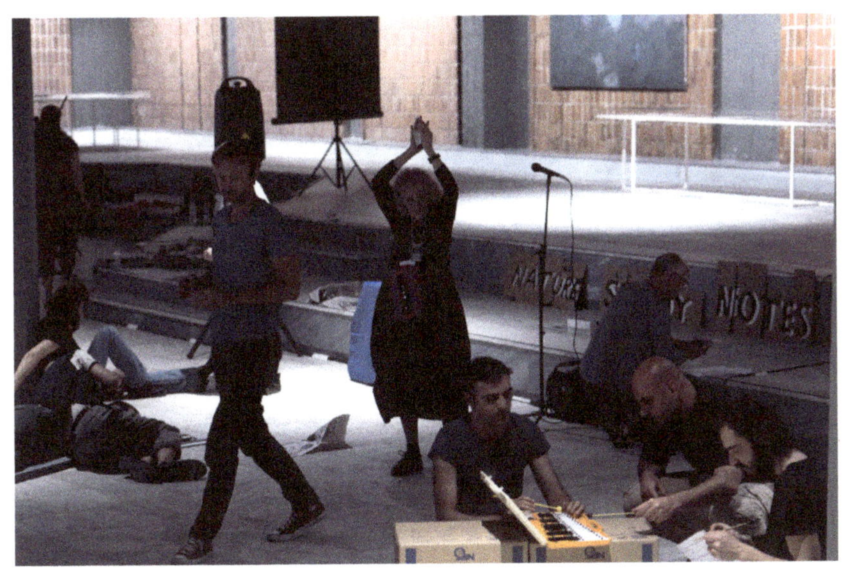
NOTES

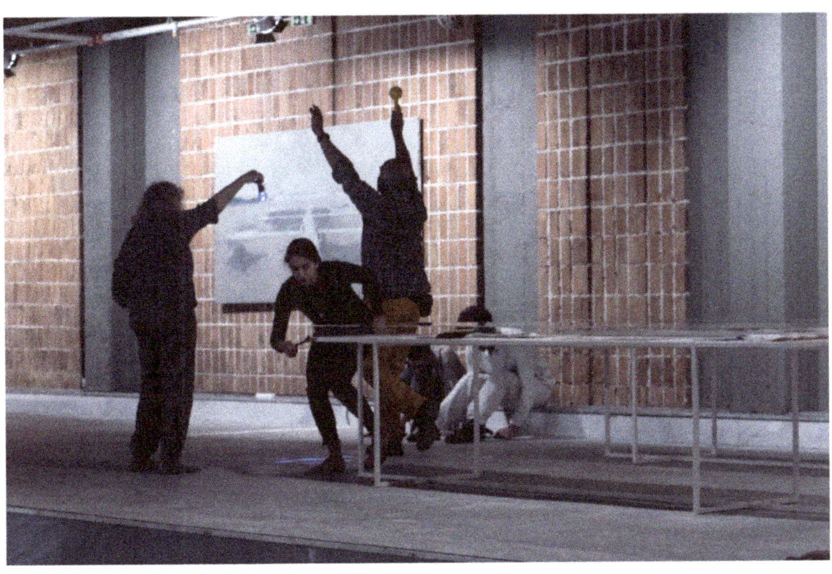

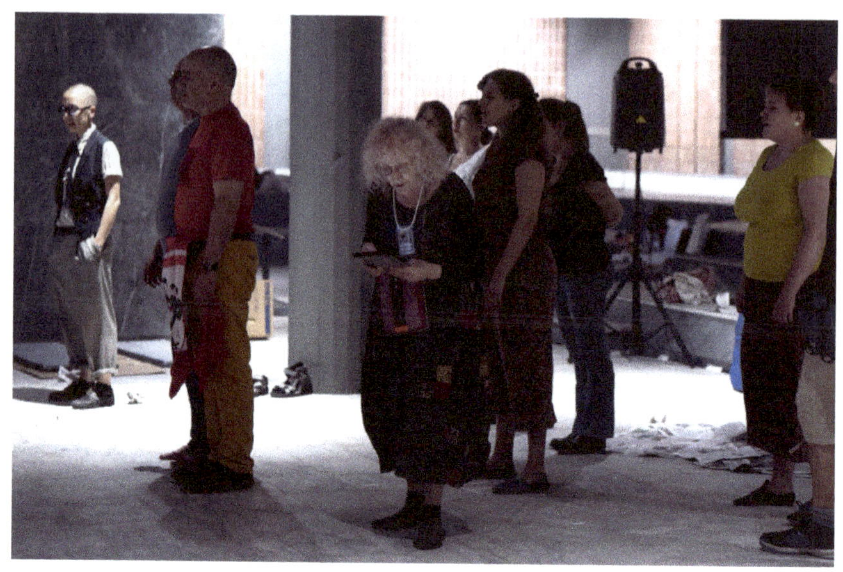

Some Conclusions

In the introduction to this chapter above I have put my thoughts on Rites as a possible means to world change. This seems a rational thought process to me, but of course the efficacy of the plan could only be proven after extensive experimental practice.

To this end the process in Athens could probably have done with another day in which we focused energy on writing new rites. It was also clear that our curator, Pierre Bal Blanc, could have done with the space for a seminar on the radical forms of composition into which he has done so much research. It is worth mentioning that we did these workshops underneath the main music academy in Athens with no participation from the musicians who were learning their craft in the floors above us. Pierre says that music academies are not interested in these kinds of scores at the current time. The Scratch Orchestra had about 70% skilled musicians. The Athens group was possibly the reverse of this. So it would have been good to have had the participation of some of the students from the academy upstairs.

There is also a limitation in considering the rites in a fine art frame. As an expressive practice their potential in contributing to change could be considered from the viewpoint of anti-psychiatry as much as aesthetics. The person I know who is thinking in this direction is Howard Slater. One of the amazing things about our Athens experience was how accessible the Nature Study Notes were. People just walked in and had a good experience in an hour or less. Because expertise is not necessary most people can experience the satisfactions of collective expression very quickly.

Our visit to other exhibits in D14 the next day

Carole and I saw the tent installed by Mounira Al Solh in the Islamic Museum. It included works and statements by Yazidi women. It was a powerful work especially in this Museum. But why hadn't the Museum or D14 painted out the racist graffitti on the wall outside.

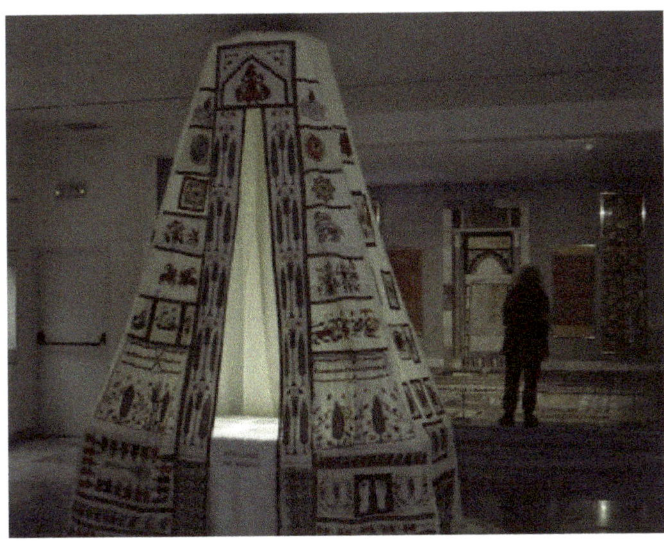

We also visited the main exhibition in the National Museum of Contemporary Art, the EMST. This shows some left-field curation with wonderful works. The projects are underpinned with thorough world-wide researches of archives, rather than just choosing predictable art stars. An example was the reconstruction of archival material relating to Arseny Avraamov's 'Symphony of Factory Sirens' in Baku 1922. https://youtu.be/Kq_7w9RHvpQ

Related to this were some images from early Soviet experiments with optical sound which filled a gap in our knowledge. Another favourite of mine was the display of archive material about Christopher D'Arcangelo a US based anarchist who challenged the gallery Art system in a way that I strongly empathised with. I knew one of the curators of this piece, Dean Inkster, who had also been instrumental in connecting with the Scratch work some years ago. http://artistsspace.org/exhibitions/christopher-darcangelo

There were 40 venues and we only saw three! The depth of the underlying curatorial research was impressive; as were other left-field perspectives and the sheer scale of the engagement with institutions in Athens. The director of Documenta, Adam Szymczyk, had been living in Athens with his family for about three years. We were told this by the taxi driver that picked us up at the airport, who also happens to take his children to school every day.

Of course, operating on this institutional level can also cause frustration to people who don't have access to these institutions. The institutions are inevitable reliant on state sources of finance and so there must be any amount of diplomatic buffering, selectivity and compromise that goes on. Cracks in this facade are offered through the inclusion of critical works like D'Arcangelo's. There is no engagement with the Squats movement or any raw engagement with the refugee crisis even though an empty building was opposite the

EMST and highly visible from the top floor balcony.

The EMST was partly empty and the lack of artwork on many walls gave the atmosphere a sense of removal from the busy life on the streets and a withdrawal into a realm of wealth and control, where space can be left empty as an insulation from the unpredictable life outside the walls. Art is inevitably a rich person's game and although Szymczyk - with his anti-fascist alliance and other manoeuvres, has done wonders - he cannot transcend the citadel that is Art. He made many radical statements which are bound to disappoint some of those on the ground. He expressed the conviction that Documenta 14 will "indeed contribute to building a bridge—a political one, over which the refugees, who need to find a safe home in Europe, might be able to walk." I have no reason to question his integrity but a complex process of symbolic adjustments to the canon over four years of work may not be able to be appreciated by mere 'day' visitors. I guess he might see himself inserting a progressive virus into the art system?

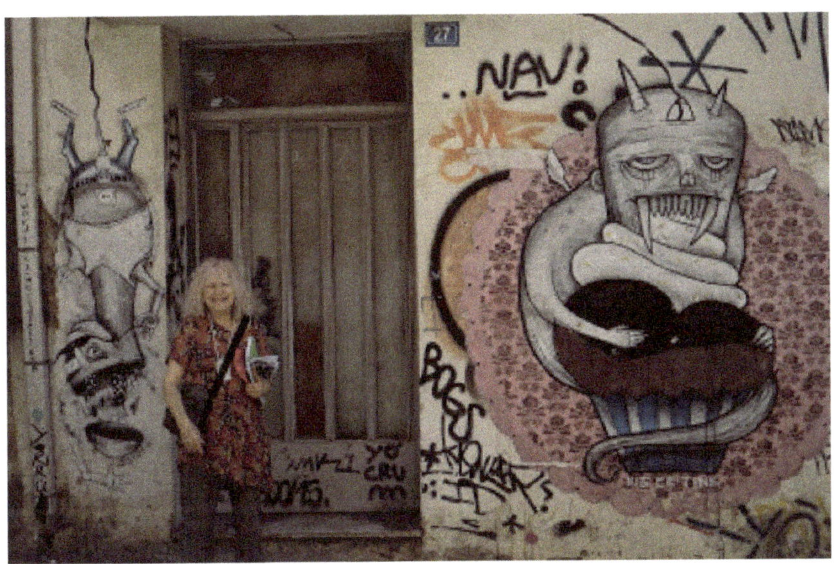

As a participating artist I felt cosseted by the luxurious hospitality given by the Documenta 14 team, at the same time as feeling grateful for it! It insulated me from the squatting movement, and as I had been squatting in London in the Eighties, and I might have felt comfortable with such contacts. It also makes it difficult for me to make a constructively critical platform from which to discuss the situation in which I found myself. Does 'Documenta Serve Imperialism' as one T-shirt we heard about playfully suggested? (One of Cardew's most famous books was; 'Stockhausen Serves Imperialism'). It is a question I did not feel I could answer as I had insufficient engagement with D14 in Athens and also knew little of its' institutional history or of the funding background of the mothership in Kassel, Germany.

I should say now that I was very pleased with the vitrine presentation that had been made of my project from 1971, The Scratch Cottage, which used 12 of my photographs and other items from the archival material I had given to MayDay Rooms. I thank those who designed and made this.

However, the original idea had been to reconstruct a 'Scratch Cottage' in the main hall in Kassel. This didn't happen. Was this because I would only agree to it being built by a group of refugees or Greek outsider artists and feared the result of it being used as a 'score' which might have rendered it too aesthetically. Anyway, the early plan for a full-scale construction fell through. I was told that a reconstruction of the original was out of the question.

Comments on the workshops from two participants

Alexandra Dami

It was a great experience to participate in the performance! I had great feeling to improvise with people that I met for the first time and making such a great team.

Carol and Stefan were very friendly and made me feel comfortable like they have been my teachers from before. Was fantastic how people from different countries, interests, professions... all together we made a group and was great the result and the feeling how a community can succeed to have communication and to be creative with a very simple way, It is powerful!

After leaving the place with the bells that Carol offered to us, ringing on my t-shit I had a very positive energy I was happy or maybe something like having had a meditation

I wish I could repeat the experience with the scratch orchestra soon!

Thanks to you all for this great experience!!! I' m looking forward to see you again!

Achilleas Karagiannidis

A really amazing opportunity to be a proud member of the three days performance of Scratch Orchestra members! Thank you from the bottom of my heart for that!!

Notes: The Documenta 14 webpage (2017) on the Scratch Orchestra has illustrations of the archive material that they displayed. http://www.documenta14.de/en/artists/16230/scratch-orchestra

Chapter 5

Conclusions

Matters arising

1. In the draft constitution of 1969 Cornelius Cardew makes it clear that members of A Scratch Orchestra are welcome to contribute rites at any time. The processes described above led to some new rites being written and performed.

2. Ali Warner devised a way that our selections of rites could easily be put online by each selector and the resulting patterns of choices seen by the whole group. Clearly this is a very different technology to what was available in the days when the rites were first used. However, it was generally felt that this technical intervention did not change the overall musical effect of the improvisations that resulted.

3. The same online spreadsheet idea was used to compile the new rites that were written as part of the process in London. Most of these new rites were not however performed. One new rite by Hugh Shrapnel, his NHS rite, was used at a subsequent Scratch Orchestra revival concert at Cafe Oto in 2017.

4. Three of the new rites, written by two women in Athens, were used in the Documenta 14 performance. This seemed to show me the probable universal utility of this written rite form. The new rites from Athens are listed below.

5. The rites have more potential than as an interesting footnote in Music History. In a world that will hopefully shed traditional religions in time, new rite creation is essential. Our Humanist history has made it seem we can live according to the written word understood silently within our heads or passively consumed. I think we need performative actions in all our sense media to express, articulate and fully evaluate common desires.

6. In this way culture can be fulfil its basic purpose of carrying out a continual and critical evaluation of our conditions in all our sense media.

Chapter 5 Section 1

ON CAGE – Tentative Conclusions

Some leading members of the Scratch Orchestra do not want to see John Cage as progenitor of the Scratch. At the beginning of this process Peter Ellison and I had gone down to see John Tilbury in his modest home on the south coast. What I'd imagined as a formal interview about Cage and his impact on the Scratch turned into a warm social occasion, and an in-depth discussion didn't really happen. But John had already written at length on John Cage in his magisterial biography of Cornelius Cardew (A Life Unfinished, 2007) and it is worth noting a few things from that book:

On the positive side

"From Cage you learn that all sounds have life, from David Tudor you learn that this life can be nourished." Cardew (25 February 1967) quoted by Tilbury p.335 2007

Cardew conceded that chance operations did, at the least, allow for more agency by the performer, so it was a significant breakthrough, but only for people who did not follow the score too closely!

"The one merit of such a purely formal score is that it releases the initiative of the performer - it gives him participation in the act of composition and hence a genuinely educative experience. In the balance on the other side is the total indifference (implicitly represented by such a formalistic score) to the seriousness of the world situation in which it occurs." (Cardew 1974 p.37)

Cage reflected the libertarian ethos of the Beat Generation with some panache. He took a vacant throne as The American modernist composer. The USA was desperate to match or surpass the cultural kudos that went with European High Modernism.

On a more critical note

Before the Scratch in1966, "In the music room of the London School of Economics AMM demonstrated an aesthetic that was a radical departure from Cage." Tilbury p.300. AMM was a smaller improvising group that Cardew was part of.

Cage surfed on the cult of the star composer within a professional music milieu (Tilbury p.608). Cardew took professional platforms offered him but often to critique those platforms, and post 1971 to use them to argue for revolution. Cage was embedded in a music hierarchy with the composer as top dog.

"Time and again Cage expressed a concern for the *inviolability* of the score". "In contrast, Cardew's music making was based on the acceptance of human vulnerability, fragility and imperfection, of contingency." Tilbury p.608

The improvisation rites arose from the collective life of The Scratch Orchestra and were written from the many viewpoints that comprised this community. They are profoundly different from an approach to music that is channeled through one mind, however diverse a work like Song Books appears to be. The rites seem to empower the intelligence of a collective and allow it to arise to the surface when they are put to work. Cage's set of instructions, partly at least, refer back to him and our fascination with his genius celebrity. It is only the few rites written by Cardew himself that could be argued to refer us to the charismatic figure he undoubtedly was.

Tilbury writes: "Cardew's eclecticism signified the deliberate destruction of the unity of the personality; the *Piano Albums* are protests against the cult of originality." Tilbury p.734

Note: Cardew himself wrote a chapter called 'Criticising Cage and Stockhausen' in his book 'Stockhausen Serves Imperialism'

Analysis from the recent praxis

In simplistic summary, Cage was into chance whereas Cardew was into choice. The performers of Song Books are meant to follow instructions which determine what they will play and when, *without reference to each other.* They then interpret the score, albeit with more leeway than with traditional scores, but still with constraints on what value judgements they could bring to bear. The songs are still channels for the great composers' intent and performers are not meant to bring too much of their own personality (creativity) into the mix.

Cardew himself saw a certain mysticism behind the strategy of using chance operations that seemed to produce originality and surprise, but this is only because performances happened within a rich elite setting, within which a lot of 'surprising' things are possible. (Tilbury p.768 footnote 51) It reminds me of the Humanists' awakening to 'mans' agency and the subsequent transcendence of fate or human submission to 'gods will'.

With The Improvisation Rites players are making all important choices. Their improvisations are not constrained in relation to the ensemble, they can respond to sounds and events around them, but also to their own innermost creative impulses. Within a concert framework they can compose and play compositions or rites in a fluid relation to the whole orchestra.

Tilbury quotes Cardew at some length about what happened if a disciplined performer (Cardew himself in this case c1960) really followed Cage's score to the letter. (Tilbury p.747. I will quote from his source, Cardew's book 'Stockhausen Serves Imperialism' (1974):

"Once Kurt Schwertsik and I, overcome with Cage's 'beautiful idea' of letting sounds be sounds (and people be people, etc., etc., in other words seeing the world as a multiplicity of fragments without cohesion), decided to do a pure performance (no gimmicks) on horn and guitar, just reading the lines and dots and notating the results and letting the sounds be themselves. The result was a desert." p.37

I had to look for 'singers' and 'electronics' musicians to form the Song Books ensemble. When using the 'Nature Study Notes' rites these 'professional' skills become unnecessary and that skill-base of the group shifted, although I still tended to invite experienced improvisers. Later in Athens, the group was open to everyone willing to take part and the result was still very satisfying. It was the experience in Athens that showed me just how accessible and relevant the rites still are.

Notes

1. Cardew has a chapter 'John Cage: Ghost or Monster?' in his book 'Stockhausen Serves Imperialism' Latimer New Directions, 1974. Republished in PDF form as one of the ubuclassics - ubu.com

2. John Tilbury also discusses Nature Study Notes improvisation rites from page 382 of 'Cornelius Cardew - A Life Unfinished' 2007

Chapter 5 Section 2

New Improvisation Rites

SS153 Fire Comes from Heaven

As preparation, an image may be drawn or downloaded.

SS154 Before coming in please wipe your feet

Metaphoric use preferred, but can be performed as an instruction as well.

SS155 Willy Nilly

Choose a jingling combination, like 'willy nilly', and make up a sentence to declaim to the audience in the manner of a street-corner orator or busker.

EW156 Speak Arabic

Speak the best Arabic you can for as long as you can. You may want to use a phrase book or an audio lesson, or repeat a few words or phrases learnt by heart.

EW157 Kiss me

Use index and thumb of both hands to clamp your mouth and jaws wide open.

Walk around saying /repeating ''Kiss me'' or "I love you" as if addressing a lover, current, past or potential; The tone and intensity may change accordingly. Stop when you feel/think that your message has got through.

LH158 Set Strategy Rite

Pair up with another person. They do not need to be doing this rite also.

Listen to their playing and pick out three parameters. (For example: pitch, speed, duration, timbre, etc.) For each of your three parameters, try to either match your partner or do the complete opposite of them.

LH159 Pop Rite

Pick any pop song which is relatively current and which contains instructions to the user on how to act, dance, sing, clap, etc, and follow these instructions outside of the song's context.

LH160 Green Rite

Reduce, re-use, recycle.

HMS161 NHS Rite

Everyone is scattered around the performing area performing any activities (rites, whatever) but awkwardly (clumsily, painfully etc.). Very gradually they leave whatever they are doing and stagger waywardly and uncertainly to an initially agreed point to slowly form a queue. When all have joined the queue, it limps/staggers around the performing area at varying speeds, directions, the performers making sounds, individually or collectively or both at different times.

Very gradually the performers one by one drop out of the queue and lie prostrate on the floor all over the performing area as far apart from each other as possible. When all are on the floor they start moaning spasmodically and softly. After 1-3 minutes a solo performer slowly attempts to get up only to sink back down again, (the other performers remaining on the floor). The solo performer repeats this a few times with greater success each time, finally managing to stagger to his/her feet. The soloist then moves to the initially agreed point and, adopting a defiant pose, fairly softly (i.e. in keeping with the overall soft dynamics) but firmly says "Save our NHS!" He/she is similarly followed by other people at an accelerating pace until everyone is standing at the point in a straight line directly facing the audience. The rite ends with all the performers, on a downbeat, shouting "Save Our NHS!"

EL162 Animal Rite

Catch a sparrow.

If they won't come to you through communication, set a trap.

Tell them that you feel love for them and that you want to tame them and be responsible for their wellbeing.

If they don't seem to understand or are showing signs of unhappiness decide to keep them in a cage or let them go.

EL163 Human Rite

Catch a human.

If it won't come to you by communication, set a trap.

Tell it that you feel love for it and that you want to tame it and be responsible for its wellbeing.

If it doesn't seem to understand or is showing signs of unhappiness decide to keep it in a cage or let it go.

EL164 Cloud Rite

Catch a cloud.

If it won't come to you through communication, set a trap.

Tell it that you feel love for it and that you want to tame it and be responsible for its wellbeing.

If it doesn't seem to understand or is showing signs of unhappiness decide to keep it in a cage or let it go.

EL165 Meateater Rite

Buy a piece of frozen meat.

Find the animal it came from.

Find which part of its body the meat came from.

Give it back.

GC166 Sweet Singing Rite

Gargle a series of recognisable tunes with a liquid of your choice.

GC167 Naive Right

Ask your mother or father* about what they think of the world today. Use their exact words in a prophetic speech or song using accompanying music of your choice. Perform with vigour and gusto.

*If mother or father not available, ask anyone you think of as older and wiser than yourself.

AWMS168 Kiss

Give someone a kiss (on the lips, possibly).

AWSS169 Write a Rite

Approach someone in the room (player or audience) and ask them to write a rite. Share some short examples if necessary. Offer them a pen and a piece of paper with the words PLEASE PERFORM THIS RITE IMMEDIATELY at the bottom. Once written, ask them to hand the rite to the player of their choice.

AWZK170 First Instrument

Consider your voice and your body movement as two indivisible elements of a single voice-body instrument (in this view, singing while remaining completely still would be like playing the piano without moving the keys). Explore making sound in this way.

AWFK171 Asymmetry is Welcome

Make a sound. Notice what you experience. Put yourself in an asymmetrical posture. Make another sound. Notice what you experience. Put another person in an asymmetrical posture (approach them gently.), while holding your own and maintaining physical contact together. Both make a sound (non-verbally invite the other person to do so). Notice what you experience. [After Frank Kane]

AWEP172 Exploration/Creation

Make free sound, experiencing your inner world as an unexplored land with many new things to discover. When inspired, feel free to leave your explorations and allow your sound-making to move into building or creating things on this land (eg. fences, walls, colourful banners that catch the wind and can be seen from afar). When inspired, feel free to leave the things you have created, and go back to discovering what is new. When inspired, feel free to go back to the things you have created, or create new ones (eg. a circle of stones around a fire, strong buildings that protect people from the elements). When inspired, feel free to return to your explorations. And so on. Consider raising a pennant or flag when you are exploring, and lowering it when you are building to help distinguish between these two modes of exploration and creation.

SS173 Txt Rite

Text someone a message from the performance space during the performance. Then copy the text message onto a sheet of paper (add a line drawing if you like). If you get a reply include that. Finally take a photo of it to share with the text recipient later.

BH174 Cough it up rite

Metaphorically: Clear your chest - the one in the attic and cellar, as well at that in your thorax. Expectorate the unexpectorated.

EZ175

Protest against the creator of the rite/ against the rite itself. Create a 'procession'/ demonstration/ riot to express your opposition.

EZ176

Take a very important decision collectively or individually. Then do the opposite to what you have decided.

EZ177

Express your gratitude to the institution (if there isn't one, then make it up).

EZ178

Breathe collectively.

EZ179

Everybody in the room uses their voice to sing a single continuous note, different than the ones sung by the people around them. The same note cannot be sung by two people. As an interval do the reverse (everybody sings the same note).

EZ180

Act Normal.

EZ181

Be the audience.

ME182

Performers move through a space. Everyone is walking/moving towards the doorsteps of change. When the performer finds his/her door, stop. Performers can only make a sound with a singular quality of any duration in lieu of knocking on this metaphorical door. The noises made must correspond to each performer's emotions vis à vis their desires for change. 1) Wait for the right moment to knock. 2) Knock right away and wait for a reply. The performance ends once everyone has knocked and feels satisfied to leave the unanswered door or feels a response emerged and walks through the door. It is not permitted to stay waiting forever.

Please Note: The numbering of these new rites follows on from the original 1969 collection.

An index of the new rite writers

AW - Ali Warner

BH - Bryn Harris

EL - Eve Libertine

EW - Emmanuelle Waeckerle

EZ - Helen 'Eleni' Zervou

GC - George Chambers

HMS - Hugh Shrapnel

LH - Les Hutchins

ME - Mika Ebbsen

SS - Stefan Szczelkun

www.ingramcontent.com/pod-product-compliance
Ingram Content Group UK Ltd.
Pitfield, Milton Keynes, MK11 3LW, UK
UKHW062302290726
14090UKWH00017B/838